Regional economic development in Italy

For Gene

Lloyd Saville

Regional economic development in Italy

Duke University Press
Durham, N.C.   1967

© 1967, Duke University Press

L.C.C. card no. 67–21707

**Printed in the United States of America
by Kingsport Press, Inc.**

Title I

Contents

III. *In summary and inference*

Map

Charts

Tables

Introduction

*For in the first place, they [the economists] deal with
facts which can be observed, and quantities which can be
measured and recorded; so that when differences of opinion
arise with regard to them, the differences can be brought to
the test of public and well-established records; and thus
science obtains a solid basis on which to work.*
— Alfred Marshall

To the economist, regional development is probably the broadest of
empirical studies. It includes not only the dimensions of time and space,
but also the sources of change in varied historical contexts. Because of
the array of facets exposed to the investigator, a relatively narrow and,
if possible, somewhat homogeneous area needs to be chosen and fre-
quent recourse made to the conventional disclaimer, *ceteris paribus.*
Although it becomes daily more unrealistic to limit the scope of inquiry
by demarking for separate analysis a single section of an increasingly
interdependent globe, the tenacious persistence of the past makes it
even more difficult to cut loose a short segment of time from all that
preceded it. Thus the constraint of delimiting the area for study to
workable proportions falls first on the feasibility of reducing the geographic extent of the inquiry. And second, it rests on sampling techniques in both time and space to hurdle the mounds of numerical
evidence found even in a restricted sphere.

Italy is the subject area. In many ways it is a single, self-contained
unit. The land occupied by the Boot, Sicily, and Sardinia is clearly
separated from other countries by mountains or the sea. The Roman
Empire, the Renaissance, and the Church were founded there and represent outstanding examples of administrative and cultural achieve-
ment. A unique language, albeit in numerous dialects, colloquialisms,
and inflections, has been spoken there generally since the time of Dante.
For these and other reasons this realm is identifiably distinct from
other areas.

In spite of this external uniformity, Italy's internal contrasts are re-
nowned. Geographically, two islands, a separating spire of mountains,

and a large plain provide at least five distinct regions. Historically, since neolithic times, successive invasions from various sources locating in diverse regions of Italy have helped to differentiate the parts of the country still further. For hundreds of years until Unification foreign powers controlled several sections of the land; the dominance of Austria over Tuscany, Spain over the Kingdom of Naples, and the Papacy over Central Italy are examples of a shifting pattern of influence. And this situation did not end with the *Risorgimento,* or final liberation of Italy in 1870. Commercial influences responding to political changes have continued external pressures ever since: France through the gateway of the Northwest, Germany by way of the Northeast, and the United Kingdom and the United States by sea and air. Early and late, each of these nations provided a special patronage to one section in particular and so imparted some of its own image to that part of Italy.

Therefore, a study of Italy is a study in contrasts—not the sort that blocks out a picture of simple white in the North and black in the South, but rather a study in shades of gray forming a complete nation. Centuries of external assaults and internecine conflicts have imbued the country with dissimilar images; it came far into the industrial revolution still doing homage to a series of foreign princelings and still paying tribute to their masters abroad.

In a sense, however, Italy is a model environment. To an original geographic and demographic situation existing a millennium ago, a variety of influences have been applied. Unique characteristics of these external forces have served to modify local conditions in many ways and to bring about wide differences in sectional levels of economic well-being. Analysis of these variations permits the identification and appraisal of their causes. A comparison of the resulting patterns of development furnishes useful evidence about the nature of Italian economic progress and provides a basis for assessing the importance of each factor influencing growth.

Any detailed examination of economic forces requires a simplified representation of the economy. Such a model need not be sophisticated to provide the necessary structure for the analysis. First, the rubrics in which to place the details of economic life in each section of the country must be delineated. Second, an approximation of the direction of the influence exerted by the more important economic forces must be ascertained. And third, some method of estimating the probable influence of future economic policies must be made available. Once a serviceable model of the economy has been outlined and the geographic sections of the country established, then the investigation can proceed to fill out the skeleton with facts drawn from the existing evidence.

Selective sampling is employed. Results obtained by probing in depth are not a listing of events or the production of all-encompassing averages for the nation as a single unit. They are, rather, measures of relative levels and directions of change experienced by each more or less unique section of the country. Such evidence and the technique employed are useful in predicting the probable effects of policy actions in the future. A section-by-section evaluation is especially instrumental because widely divergent levels of development often call for dissimilar policy prescriptions. Thus, economic policies in the past and in the future can be appraised both for the economy as a whole and for each of its constituent parts.

Any one book, regardless of its size, which seeks to cover even a single aspect of an entire nation must do so selectively. Because of its illustrious past and present diversity, Italy should be examined with great discretion. The technique of the zoom lens or the exploratory operation, in one case focuses on critical features, leaving out much of the action, or in the other examines concealed problems while hopefully preserving the health of the patient. The sampling technique and the choice of topics used in the present study disregard much valuable information and investigate only a limited number of subjects. Insight is thus gained into contrasting situations of prime relevance to regional economic development.

So that the study may be readily understood by as wide an audience as possible, technical terms, even the economic ones, are held to a minimum. For the same reason, English works and translations have been cited where possible. In the use of the British and American sources there is an added gain in perspective often found in foreign commentaries. The Italian equivalents of English terms are shown in some cases to avoid ambiguity regarding the exact source of each statistic and to enable a student unfamiliar with the Italian vocabulary to bridge the gap of language to the numbers themselves.

This study was made possible by encouragement and help from the Research Council of Duke University, the Ford Foundation, the Guggenheim Foundation, and the State Department. Many librarians, archivists, and officials aided materially with the acquisition of data and its arrangement in a semblance of order. Demanding a special note of the kindness shown in many instances by their willingness not only to permit, but also to provide facilities for, the microfilming of records were: in Rome those at the Vatican, the Ministry of Finance, the Ministry of Labor and Social Security, the Chamber of Deputies, the State Archives, the Institute for the Industrial Development of the South, the Central Institute of Statistics, the General Federation of Italian Industry, and the National Central Library; in Naples at the State Archives and the National Library; in Florence at the State Archives and the National Central Library; in Pisa at the State Archives and the University Library; in Milan at the State Archives and the National Brera Library; in Turin at the City, National, and University libraries; in Venice at the National Marcia Library; in Paris at the National Archives; in Madrid at the University Library; near Valladolid at the General Archives of Simanca; in London at the British Museum; in Boston at the Boston Public Library; in New York City at the New York Public Library; and in Washington at the Library of Congress and the National Archives. The staff at the Duke University Library have been unstinting in their efforts to be of assistance. My thanks are due also to the editors of the *Economic History Review* and the *Southern Economic Journal* for permission to use parts of articles originally published in their pages.

Deserving special thanks for their guidance and forbearance are my colleagues at Duke University, especially Professor Frank T. de Vyver and Dr. Athos Ottolenghi, who have read much of the manuscript, and those at the Graduate Institute for European Studies at Turin during the academic year 1959–1960, particularly Dr. Gustavo Malan and Dr. Carlo Cippola who acquainted me with many aspects of the Italian scene. In addition, Dr. George H. Hildebrand deserves special mention for his careful reading and helpful suggestions. Mrs. Thelma Keene's painstaking and skilful typing of the manuscript is gratefully acknowledged. In spite of this assistance, responsibility for the inaccuracies that persist is my own. This study would not have been started in the first place and certainly would not have been continued to completion had it not been for the wholehearted support and concord given to it by my wife, Gene, and for the tolerance and sympathy accorded by my children, Curt and Lynn; for they are the ones who pay much of the price of individual inquiry, gain little of its pleasures, and share only indirectly in its rewards.

I. *The problem, its milieu and scope*

1. *The rubrics of change*

> *Development in our sense is a distinct phenomenon, entirely foreign to what may be observed in the circular flow or in the tendency towards equilibrium. It is spontaneous and discontinuous change in the channels of the flow, disturbance of equilibrium, which forever alters and displaces the equilibrium state previously existing.*
> — Joseph Schumpeter

Some crucial factors

From the wattle huts in the area of the Forum at the time of Romulus to the pastel apartment houses on the Parioli in modern Rome is only some two miles in space, but some twenty-seven hundred years in time and an eon in economic development. The change in the material wellbeing of the people is evidenced not only in the improvement in housing, but also in the skill with which the dwellings are kept. Stratified layers of refuse embedded in the floors by the sketchy housekeeping of successive generations of Villanovan housewives contrast with the high gloss achieved by the regular application of polishing pads by modern housekeepers. Beyond the increase in physical advantages and the ability to put them to use, there is also some change in the way these advantages are shared by the group. In primitive societies, others than the warrior, the priest, and the tribal chief may receive fewer economic advantages, less food, poorer housing, or be denied the privilege of wearing certain ornaments; today, squatters who live in shacks on the side of the Parioli receive a lower share of total income than those who live above in luxury apartments. These are several reflections of economic development—the capacity to produce more goods and services in total, the ability to use this increasing total more efficiently, and the willingness to distribute this total more effectively.

Responsible in part for such improvements in wellbeing are the enlarged stock of capital plant and equipment, an expanded availability of natural and human resources, a vast extension in the store of knowledge, a much enhanced educational system, and an exceedingly more

3

complex economic and social establishment. Changes wrought in these
and other areas, then, determine the economic wellbeing of the country and its people. The subject categories are very broad, and an exhaustive list of influential factors is distressingly long. In order to limit
the scope of inquiry to workable dimensions choice needs to be made
among the vast array of factors influential in determining economic development. The question in order becomes: What forces in the Italian
economy have been most noteworthy in bringing about the development
from primitive tribes to an economically advanced nation?

To answer this question a simple model can be used. The factors
of production—land, labor, capital, know-how—and the established
framework of the existing social order provide the needed headings.[1] It is clear that within the relevant area of usual experience,
ceteris paribus, an increase in the quantity or the quality of any one
of these will produce a larger product.[2] Thus in colonial United States
the inflow of capital, people, and knowledge; the increased availability
of raw materials; and the development of bigger markets all helped
to produce a larger product. Each of these factors contributed positively to economic growth.

After this initial development in a new country has passed, increased
attention is usually required by the government. In order to take advantage of the economies of scale, markets must be increased in size.
In order to provide for efficient exchange, especially at a distance, a
money and banking system must be provided. And, in order to limit
the restrictive actions of monopolies, controls must be introduced. Examples of attempts by the state to fulfill this obligation are found in
the granting of subsidies for the construction of railroads, highways,
and airports; in providing currency and creating a banking structure;
and in making laws controlling trusts, cartels, and coercive organiza-

---

1. Note that the first German edition of Joseph A. Schumpeter's *The Theory of Economic
Development* appeared in 1912. The English version was translated by R. Opie (Cambridge:
Harvard University Press, 1949). Irma Adelman, *Theories of Economic Growth and Development* (Stanford: Stanford University Press, 1961), pp. 9 and 95, suggests the following
generalized form of Schumpeter's production function:
$$Y = f(K, N, L, S, U)$$
where
    Y is output, L is labor force,
    K is produced means of production, S is society's fund of applied knowledge, and
    N is natural resources, U is "the social-cultural milieu."
2. That is, up to the limiting point of zero marginal physical product which does not
seem to be reached even in the most populous backward areas. See Harry Oshima,
"Underemployment in Backward Economies—An Empirical Comment," *Journal of
Political Economy,* LXVI (1958), p. 259.

tions. These are elementary economic and social facilities needed to disencumber the functioning of this simple economy. To the extent that these responsibilities are adequately performed, growth is enhanced; to the extent that they are not, growth is impaired.

As the economic and social order becomes more complex new problems are generated. Not only have variables been added, the relative importance of each of them has been altered. The primary new issue is employment. With it come the associated issues of saving and investment and the panoply of multipliers, accelerators, and gaps; but most important is the altered role of the state.[3] Its relatively passive function during the early stages of development will no longer suffice. The increased intricacy of the economic order requires an active participation by the state both to insure a wide range of employment opportunities and to encourage a viable level of economic growth. This responsibility may become appreciably more complex as higher levels of industrialization are reached and increasingly unstable situations evolve from the interactions of saving, investment, and expectations.[4]

In reality, economic development can take a number of forms. Two distinct examples may be considered. First is the evolution of the development process for the country as a whole in an open frontier environment. The components of growth outlined above were couched in this setting; Australia, New Zealand, and the United States exemplify the type. They were settled during a period of rapid industrial change and political upheaval.[5] In these areas there was little indigenous population. The newly introduced population was conditioned to change by the very fact of its immigration. There was no established order; the new one was founded by diverse and sometimes dissident groups.

Not so the Italian development; it passed through the frontier stage at the time of the wattle huts. Italy provides an example of a second form which economic development may take. A firmly established eco-

3. A citation to the "new economics" of the later thirties and forties is in order here. Beginning, of course, with Keynes, it should also list Hansen, Duesenberry, Modigliani, Klein, Katona, and many others.

4. Arguments relating to the Harrod-Domar thesis are relevant here, especially Roy F. Harrod, "An Essay in Dynamic Theory," *Economic Journal*, XLIX (1939), pp. 14–33; Evsey D. Domar, "Expansion and Employment," *American Economic Review*, XXXVII (1947), pp. 34–55; and Roy F. Harrod, *Toward a Dynamic Economics* (London: Macmillan, 1948), pp. 63–100. The point to be emphasized is the possibility of disruptive fluctuations in employment and income being engendered by the ungoverned play of complex economic forces.

5. See, for example, Everett E. Hagen, *On the Theory of Social Change* (Homewood, Illinois: Dorsey Press, 1962), for a general statement.

nomic and social order was in place prior to each modern advance. Because of the large and densely settled resident population, the careful regulation of commercial activity by guilds, the only recent emancipation from feudalism in many sections, and the wide temporal and almost universal spiritual power of a single church, the prevailing order was confirmed. Thus, before any change could be introduced the already existing regulations needed to be altered. In this way an additional obstacle was placed in the way of growth. In the open-territory situation, a new device could be adopted as soon as its need was felt. But in this closed-territory case, the existing practice had to be disarmed before a new one could be installed in its place.

Pressing the analysis, a further level of sophistication is evident. The latent assumption that development occurs everywhere within the country at the same time is withdrawn. In Italy and perhaps in most countries, progress is not uniformly spread throughout the nation; rather it advances in some parts while it remains relatively stable or even regresses in others. France and the United States are cases in point. In economic terms Paris and its immediate environs have forged notably ahead of the rest of France. Included within the capital's urban complex are the manufacturing, marketing, educational, governmental, artistic, transportation, and tourist centers of all France.[6] In the southern United States development has been significantly slower than in the rest of the country. Family size, industry mix, facility segregation, and adherence to the status quo all tend to make average incomes lower in this one region in comparison with others.[7] In Italy the North-South dichotomy is traditional and leads to the problem of dealing with two different segments of the same line of economic development simultaneously. When diverse developmental levels exist within a nation, another problem becomes evident. Dissimilar levels require dissimilar techniques for encouragement. A prescription for growth in colonial America is quite different from a stimulant for progress in the United States today. Separate diagnosis and treatment for each region is essential for viable

---

6. Effects of this geographic phenomenon on wages, for example, may be seen in Philippe Madinier, *Les disparités, géographiques de salaries en France* (Paris: Librairie Armand Colin, 1959).

7. C. B. Hoover and B. U. Ratchford, *Economic Resources and Policies of the South* (New York: Macmillan Company, 1951), pp. 19–29; Lloyd Saville, "Earnings of Skilled and Unskilled Workers in New England and the South," *Journal of Political Economy*, LXII (1954), pp. 390–405; and his "Regional Contrasts in the Development of Local Public Finance," *National Tax Journal*, XV (1962), pp. 155–69.

economic growth. In terms of policy, the result is perplexing, since the remedy for one may be the scourge of the other.

Economic growth within a nation, then, may be concerned with two dissimilar aspects of the same basic problem. In one case the question may have to do with finding ways to engender material progress in an underdeveloped area. In another instance the issue may concern highly industrialized sections which need to find ways of fostering the continued realization of acceptable levels of expansion.[8] Since the conditions of economic success merge one with another over a considerable line of flanking skirmishes, bringing both advances and retreats, these two aspects of the problem are parts of the same wavering sequence of progress.

In response to such a situation where widely separated levels of development exist side by side within the same nation, a concept of dualism has evolved.[9] The national labor force is looked upon as being made up of two parts, the advanced and the retarded. Pakistan is an example of the situation existing in many countries where both segments compete within the same market; there the cottage system of cigarette making functions beside the machinery-using factory section. Italy, too, is plagued by this dichotomy. The prosperous Sicilian system of textile production competed, if unsuccessfully, with the factory system of its Lombardian counterpart. Then, too, there is decidedly a problem of space. The relative immobility of the labor factor makes the circumstance akin to a problem in international trade in which national barriers are replaced by those of distance, background, education, and tradition. Before turning to the evidence itself, some notion of the relative importance of the major influences on the growth of both underdeveloped and developed economies is indicated.

Ordering these factors

Even provisional ranking of these items should have some perspective in fact. An appropriate source for preliminary use is a series of studies of United States development. Although these results apply to a differ-

8. Note stress on the point of different situations and different diagnoses in J. K. Galbraith, *Economic Development in Perspective* (Cambridge: Harvard University Press, 1962), p. 12.

9. Vera Lutz has used this analytical device extensively in her treatment of Italian economic growth, *Italy: A Study in Economy Development* (Oxford: Oxford University Press, 1962); see especially pp. 13–42.

ent country, the importance of each has changed only modestly over
the recent past. Thus, arranging the variables in this fashion may not be
too remote from the reality of most areas.

Over the past quarter of a century, growth in the United States has
resulted more from advances in productivity than from increases in the
quantity of labor and the volume of capital. Kendrick, Solow, Knowles,
and the Bureau of Labor Statistics all concur in this fact.[10] It can thus
be assumed provisionally that development in many situations arises
primarily from increases in the quality of factors. A better trained and
motivated labor force, a higher level of machine efficiency, and an improved allocation of resources, materials, and markets are all indications
of greater proficiency rather than simply larger amounts of the
same factors of production. Of course, the United States' economy dif-
fers from Italy's, and the ordering of the headings may also differ;
however, the importance of improvements in quality as opposed to improvements in quantity should not be neglected, especially in the industrial regions of Northern Italy.

Denison suggests that the combined contribution of increases in quantity of labor and increases in quantity of capital accounts for only about
one third of recent growth in the United States.[11] Since the size of the
labor force is increasing less rapidly than the population, in per capita
terms there has been a net loss in the labor input.[12] Furthermore, the
expansion of capital at times has been confined to equipping the new
entrants into the labor force with tools equal to those of persons already
working.[13] In spite of this, during most years of the recent past capital
expansion has competed successfully with population growth and has
provided a deepening as well as a widening of capital.

Unemployment is, of course, a deterrent to growth. Mills found that
some 9 per cent of potential income in the United States in the first
half of the twentieth century was engrossed by unemployment, a larger

10. John W. Kendrick in Joint Economic Committee, *Relationship of Prices to Economic
Stability and Growth*, 85th Congress, 2nd Session (1958), pp. 99–125; Robert M. Solow,
"Technical Change in the Aggregate Production Function," *Review of Economics and
Statistics*, XXXIX (1957), pp. 312–20, especially p. 319; U.S. Bureau of Labor Statistics,
Bulletin No. 1249, *Trends in Output Per Man-Hour in the Private Economy, 1909–58* (Wash-
ington: U.S. Government Printing Office, 1957); James W. Knowles, *The Potential
Economic Growth of the United States*, Study Paper No. 20, Joint Economic Committee,
86th Congress, 2nd Session (1960), pp. 34–35.
11. Edward F. Denison, *The Sources of Economic Growth in the United States* (New York:
Committee for Economic Development, 1962), pp. 264–74.
12. Knowles, *op. cit.*, p. 33.
13. *Ibid.*, p. 42.

amount than was expended in total on both World War I and World War II.[14] More recent estimates by Knowles [15] indicate that each 1 per cent unemployment in the labor force in association with related growth variables accounts for roughly one twentieth of potential growth. Thus, unemployment may engulf substantial gains from other causes.

A more systematic enumeration of the sources of economic growth is in order. In a given situation of natural endowments, development comes about almost equally from three broad categories: labor, capital, and organization. In labor the quantity increase matches the quality increase almost exactly. In capital the same situation prevails. In organization the origins of progress spread over innovations in technology, resource allocation, and the use of raw materials, plus the economies of scale stemming from broader and deeper markets.[16]

But this begs the solution by employing such general terms that appropriate empirical evidence is wanting. As noted above, the labor determinant involves both quantity and quality elements. To the extent that the greater quantity of the labor factor evolves from a larger population there may be a gain in total product, but not necessarily one in per capita product. From the point of view of the individual the latter criterion is the more valid. Therefore the relative changes in the numbers of the labor force arising from higher employment rates and from the proportion of the population gainfully employed are more significant indicators of the quantity of labor than simple changes in its number. In Italy, for example, 55 per cent of the total population were included in the labor force in 1871, while this number had dwindled to 41 per cent by 1964.[17]

In a similar way the influences of each of the other factors may be broken down into workable pieces. The quality of labor is improved by advances in training and by strengthening of physical capabilities. Formal education and general, vocational, and on-the-job training play

14. Frederick C. Mills, "Technological Gains and Their Uses," *Science*, CV (1947), pp. 220–23.
15. Knowles, *op. cit.*, pp. 40–41.
16. This would modify the Schumpeterian formulation noted earlier to

$$\frac{dY}{dt} = \frac{\partial f}{\partial L}\frac{dL}{dt} + \frac{\partial f}{\partial K}\frac{dK}{dt} + \frac{\partial f}{\partial O}\frac{dO}{dt},$$

where dO is change in organization and dL, dK, and dO are each of roughly the same magnitude. See Adelman, *op. cit.*, p. 95.
17. Associazione per lo Sviluppo dell'Industria nel Mezzogiorno (hereinafter cited as SVIMEZ), *Statistiche sul mezzogiorno d'Italia, 1861–1953* (Rome: Stabilimento Tipografico Fausto Failli, 1954), pp. 978–79; and Istituto Centrale di Statistica, *Annuario di statistiche provinciali: 1963* (Rome: Azienda Beneventana Tipografica Editoriale, 1963), p. 978.

roles in this regard and find measure in changes in the relative number
of the population and the duration of their exposure to these activities.
Measurements of stature, chest, and biceps give a crude indication of the
physical status of the population. And there have been definite gains
here. In the heights of conscripts, those with a birth year of 1854 showed
only sixty-four inches on the average, while those born seventy-five
years later measured a full two inches taller.[18] Inexplicit as such figures are for the questions to be answered, they do at least give some
numerical evidence of the direction of change.

In the realm of capital other measures are available. Expansion of
the quantity of capital depends in part for its effect on the growth of
the labor force. As each new worker becomes gainfully employed he must
be equipped with tools and facilities up to the level of those already
working. This widening of capital provides an expansion in gross product but no advance to the individual. It is only by increasing the tools
used by each worker, both old and new, that a deepening of capital
occurs, and it is only by a deepening of capital that per capita growth
takes place. Thus a measure of capital available to each worker needs
careful review. Such a measure showed an increase over the decade
from 1952 to 1961 as investment per worker in Italy grew by two million lire, or an equivalent of some thirty-two hundred dollars.[19] Thereby
more tools were provided to the old as well as the new members of the
labor force.

But no one of the available statistical series is satisfactory by itself.
This is especially true of those giving data at the regional level. Several
measures, however, which are inadequate individually, provide effective
evidence of the degree of capital deepening if they are used simultaneously as a group. Variations in the amount of capital invested in industry per worker, alterations in the motive power employed in industry
per worker, modifications in the usable mileage of highways and railroads per square mile, and related series show an indication of the
movement of this important title. Such an indication does not, of
course, distinguish between shifts in the quantity of capital and varia-

18. Computed from Ministero dell'Interno, Direzione Generale di Statistica, *Annuario
statistico italiano: 1874* (Rome: Tipografia Elzeviriana, 1878), Parte prima, pp. 72–75;
and Istituto Centrale di Statistica, *Annuario statistico italiano: 1953* (Rome: Istituto Poligrafico dello Stato, 1954), p. 34.
19. Derived from *Annuario statistico italiano: 1953*, p. 330; *1960*, p. 370; *1961*, pp. 332
and 388; and *1963*, p. 402.

tions in the quality of capital. It tends instead to become a composite of both.

Organization, the third variable, covers a broad area. Ranging widely in both the private and the public spheres, it encompasses innovations in management techniques, advances in the use of resources, progress in enlarging markets through improvements in communications and reductions in political barriers, lessening of frictions impeding the free movement of the factors of production, and cultivation of an environment conducive to change.

Since the field is so wide, obtaining a numerical measure of this variable is extremely difficult. Some intimation may be obtained from such indicators as advances by minor religious sects, migration of population between areas, promotion of the creative arts, reduction in the length of residence required for social services, and enlargement of telephone, telegraph, and postal traffic. For instance, interurban telephone messages have almost doubled over the past five years and have increased more than tenfold since World War II.[20] Even though this is a remarkable growth, it provides only an oblique view of the multifaceted question of organizational development.

Furthermore, it is in this broad area that the aspects of demand enter the analysis. The literature, both theoretical and empirical, emphasizes the problems of production rather than those of consumption. The often unstated assumption seems to be that the acts of investment and production will provide employment, and consequently the wherewithal to convert latent demand into effective demand and thus clear the market of all goods and services. Because this is the general assumption, when persistent difficulties arise the public sector is expected to provide an ever-expanding market in the form of defense contracts, subsidy payments, living allowances, and the like. Expanding demand in the private sector as a means of providing fuller employment and more active growth is a possibility to be considered.

In the ensuing chapters, once the regions of the country have been demarcated and the scope of the market has been detailed, numerical evidence regarding three major rubrics is considered. The first is labor, which encompasses the crucial issues of population and education. The second is capital, which is currently favored in the materialistic approach to economic development. The third is organization, which

20. *Annuario statistico italiano: 1949–50*, p. 283; and *1965*, p. 299.

covers a wide variety of more or less related influences. Of especial importance under this diverse heading is the influence of social mores, of the attitude of the Church, and of the posture of the state. This last is crucial in providing a fertile environment for competitive market forces; fostering the acceptance of change in the form of new methods, materials, products, and services; and enlightening all of the people concerning the costs as well as the rewards of growth.

Since Italy is a member of the European Economic Community, it is subject to the changing competitive forces engendered by the mutual reduction of tariffs in the Common Market. For this reason the status of Italy and its regions is measured at certain critical places against this broader market. Since education is such a decisive issue in economic development, it is examined in two places—both in its labor factor context and as a facet of investment. Also, since Italian regions were occupied by a number of foreign powers, each section reveals unmistakable evidence of these external forces. In reviewing state control, concentration on the more recent past is discarded and a plunge in depth is taken in order to show some results of century after century of foreign administrations.

Before turning to the analysis itself attention is given in the next chapter to refining the concept of the regions of Italy. This should facilitate a more complete understanding of the role of diverse local forces in economic development and of the way these forces engender uneven progress.

2. The divisions of Italy

*If everything occurred at the same time there would be
no development. If everything existed in the same place there
could be no particularity. Only space makes possible the particular, which then unfolds in time.*

— August Lösch

Seven diverse regions

Set off from easy access by mountains and sea, the peninsula and
islands of Italy seem invulnerable. Yet as early as paleolithic times there
began a colonizing by some peoples and a conquering by others. Even
the first of these invasions still bears fruit as persistent variations in customs, tolerances, and practices from the past produce differences in
levels of economic wellbeing in the present.

Current usage divides Italy into a number of sectional arrangements.
A simple North-South dichotomy is common in questions concerning the
underdeveloped Mezzogiorno.[1] A three-way division into an industrial
Northwest encompassing Turin, Genoa, and Milan, an agricultural
Northeast embracing the rest of the country to just below Rome, and
the traditional South which includes the islands has been employed recently by the Central Institute of Statistics.[2] The Italian Constitution
specifies four sections, North, Central, South, and Insular; and even
this division combines unlike elements. Long domination and influence
by foreign forces and temporal control by the Church have left divergent patterns of economic thought and practice in various regions. Likewise, the very presence of islands, especially Sardinia, which is large and
remote from the Mainland, presents a barrier to the national unification
of diverse regional peculiarities and a great variability in the statistical
measures describing the country as a whole. Because of these influences,
the economic mores of Italy today reflect, both positively and negatively,

1. See, for example, Shepard B. Clough and Carlo Livi, "Economic Growth in Italy:
An Analysis of the Uneven Development of North and South," *Journal of Economic History*,
XVI (1956), pp. 334–49.
2. Istituto Centrale di Statistica, "Primi studi sui conti economici territoriali,"
Annali di statistica, Series 8, XII (1960).

complex groups of human and natural elements, and create a sectionalism requiring a more detailed differentiation than even the four legally
constituted sections.

Fundamental geographical and historical facts demarcate seven relatively homogeneous areas. Northern Italy can be subdivided into Northwest and Northeast; the Central section into Tuscany and East Central;
the South maintained as it has been; and the Insular separated into
Sicily and Sardinia. Although the number of sections is increased by
three, the resulting division has sufficient historical validity and social
cohesiveness to be used as a basis for sampling.

Variations in social characteristics distinguish these regions of Italy.
Although pertinent statistical evidence is of varied date and accuracy,
some numerical measures of sectional differences corroborating the facts
of political history can be derived. The first full year of Italy's complete
unification, 1871, is an appropriate starting point, i.e., the moment when
all of the complex regional forces were brought together in one nation,
but before the powers of national unity could begin to adapt local idio-
syncrasies into a uniform national pattern.

From section to section great differences were evident in cardinal
economic facts. Even the few statistical series available for all sections
of the country show the scope of this regionalism. Except on the island
of Sardinia, population density was high and relatively uniform (Table
1). Community size, a crude standard of market scope, varied widely
from the large areas of Tuscany to the small ones in the Northwest and
Northeast. Educational attainment, as indicated by reading ability,
and political preference, as displayed by the franchised 2 per cent of
the population, assess respectively a crucial utilization of economic gain
and a measurable response to environmental conditions. In both reading
ability and political preference, North-South cleavages were apparent.
By all of these broad measures each of the seven geographic sections
exhibited a dissimilar economic heritage.

Sardinia. Geographically the sharpest division between parts of Italy
arises from the distance over water separating Sardinia from the Mainland and Sicily. After an uncertain early settlement, Sardinia passed
from one domination to another—Carthaginian, Roman, Pisan, Spanish, and Austrian. It was then incorporated, with the Piedmont, into the
Kingdom of Sardinia (1720). Sardinia is thus distinguished from Sicily

by this special background and by the lack of direct communication between the two. Plagued by malaria until only recently, Sardinia shows
its uniqueness by each of the statistical measures, but most especially
by a density of population that was less than a third as great as the
Mainland average and an educational system that produced one reader
among seven persons in 1871.

Table 1. *Certain social characteristics of sections of Italy shortly after national
Unification*

	North-west	North-east	Tus-cany	East Central	South	Sicily	Sar-dinia	Italy
Density of population, average number of persons per square mile, 1871	280	315	231	191	218	228	68	234
Size of community, average in square miles, 1871	7	8	33	19	18	31	26	14
Reading ability, per cent of persons aged 6 and over able to read, 1871	55	42	32	25	17	15	14	31
Political preference, per cent of vote for Right party, 1874	70	70	77	69	33	14	53	54

Source: Computed from Ministero di Agricoltura, Industria e Commercio, Ufficio
Centrale di Statistica, *Popolazione presente ed assente per comuni, centri e frazioni di comune,
Censimento 31 dicembre 1871*, I, Parte seconda (Rome: Stamperia Reale, 1874), pp. 303–5;
and II (Rome: Stamperia Reale, 1875), pp. B, C, F, G, H, and L; Ministero dell'Interno,
Direzione Generale di Statistica, *Annuario statistico italiano: 1878* (Rome: Stamperia Reale,
1878), Parte prima, pp. 30–31; and Istituto Centrale Statistica e Ministero per la
Costituente, *Compendio delle statistiche elettorali italiane dal 1848 al 1934* (Rome: Istituto
Poligrafico dello Stato, 1947), II, pp. 120–22.

Sicily. Ethnically the greatest cleavage occurs between the Northern
Mainland and Sicily. The paleolithic migrations from Africa took two
major routes, one crossing to Spain and following the arc along the
Riviera to Italy and the second making use of the then still apparent
row of islands and reefs to Sicily. The first never seems to have extended
its influence below Tuscany, the second never much above Naples.[3]
Thus, the North-South split has roots as early as prehistoric tribal
migrations.

Separation of Sicily from the Mainland at the Straits of Messina was

3. David Randall-MacIver, *Italy Before the Romans* (Oxford: Clarendon Press, 1928),
pp. 17–18.

definitive; cultural influences stemmed from the whole Mediterranean world, as they did on the Southern Boot; but Insular status and internal dichotomy augmented different political involvements to render Sicily a separate entity.[4] Within the island itself, Crete and the Eastern Mediterranean predominated in the past of the eastern half; Iberia and the Arabic regions dominated the western part. Modern reflections of how these varied forces congealed to make Sicily quite distinct from the rest of Italy are seen in Table 1. The island shares a large community size with Tuscany and a low proportion of readers with Sardinia and the South, but showed a unique preference for the political Left. This may reflect more a dislike of the party in power and the existing economic order than any real preference for the Left *per se*.[5]

South. Third of the relatively less developed sections, the South includes the five compartments of the peninsula below Rome: Abruzzi and Molise, Campania, Puglia, Basilicata, and Calabria. Insulated by distance from the many invasions that harassed the North, and by the whirlpool of Charybdis from the influences of Sicily, it was an area less conducive to development than others in Italy. The effort was too great for the invaders from the North; although the lush fields of Metaponte did attract the Greeks and the haven at Paestum was a key colony in the trade between the homeland and the Etruscans,[6] both of these were dwarfed by the installations at Taormina, Syracuse, Agrigento, Selinunte, and Segeste. The South early boasted extraordinarily rich farm lands, a leading center of industry at Capua, and a place of commerce and culture at Pompeii.[7] In 1871, however, as the results of such developments as three hundred years of Spanish domination, a modernizing half-century of French rule, and the restoration of Spanish control with the armed assistance of Austria, it showed a low standard of reading ability and an apparent aversion to the political Right (Table 1).

4. *Ibid.*, pp. 147–57; T. E. Peet, *The Stone and Bronze Ages in Italy* (Oxford: Clarendon Press, 1909), pp. 200–39 and 432–91; and V. G. Childe, *The Dawn of European Civilization* (6th ed.; New York: Knopf, 1958), pp. 229–51.

5. Six years later, for example, the division of the returns between Right and Left were 46 per cent to 54 per cent, for then the Lefts were in office. Istituto Centrale di Statistica e Ministero per la Costituente, *Compendio delle statistiche elettorali italiane dal 1848 al 1934* (Rome: Istituto Poligrafico dello Stato, 1947), II, pp. 120–21.

6. Raymond Bloch, *The Etruscans* (London: Thames and Hudson, 1958), p. 93 (this is a revised and expanded version of his *Le mystère étrusque* translated by Stuart Hood), and David Randall-MacIver, *The Etruscans* (Oxford: Clarendon Press, 1927), pp. 1–17.

7. Tenny Frank, *Rome and Italy of the Republic*, Vol. I of Tenny Frank, T. R. S. Broughton, R. G. Collingwood, A. Grenier, *et al.* (eds.), *An Economic Survey of Ancient Rome* (6 vols.; Baltimore: Johns Hopkins Press, 1933), pp. 175–79 and 282; and David Randall-MacIver, *Greek Cities in Italy and Sicily* (Oxford: Clarendon Press, 1931), pp. 7, 8, 12–13, and 74.

THE SEVEN
REGIONS
OF ITALY

Contrasting with these three less developed Insular and Southern sections are the four more advanced regions in the North. Unlike those areas in which ethnic characteristics have remained relatively static since the Neolithic Age, the four northerly regions have been altered by repeated invasions. Although there are no differences so immediately apparent as those of an island or an extremity of a peninsula among the Northern regions, they are identifiable as distinct geographic areas. They are identified by the way the market for most goods and services is self-contained and separated from the markets of other areas more by barriers of custom, law, or other resistance to the flow of economic activity than by the previously encountered natural phenomena. Nevertheless, in each case the scope of the market generally turns in upon itself for the great bulk of all exchange.

Northwest. Early statistical compilations distinguish as Piemontese [8] the whole area now comprising the regions of the Piedmont, the Valley of Aosta, and Liguria. A continuation of this older classification is logical. The ancient Ligurian settlement, the Gaulish invasion, the proximity to modern France, the unity of the house of Savoy, the long and effective opposition to the Austrians, and the dominance of the great Cavour distinguish this area from Lombardy and the other Northeastern states. By the statistical measures shown in Table 1 the Northwest is unique. In 1871 a substantially larger proportion of the population in this section responded that they could read than in any other region. In comparison with the Northeast, population was slightly less dense, and communities were even smaller in area—the smallest in Italy and only about one-fifth as large, on the average, as those in Tuscany.

Northeast. From ancient times subject to Bohemian influence and lying between further developed cultures to the north, south, and east, the Lombardy-Venetia area was subjected to a persistent and thoroughgoing occupation from which border provinces to the north and east have only recently been released. This whole region shares a common background of Austrian influence. The situation is not as clear in the area now making up the province of Emilia-Romagna, for the Romagna region was long a part of the Papal States (1278–79 to 1860). To avoid the almost impossible bookkeeping problem of dividing the statistics of

8. For example, Ministro delle Finanze, *Relazione delle amministrazioni finanziarie* (Rome: Tipografia Cooperativa Sociale, 1874), p. 134.

a single compartment between two areas, this refinement has been disregarded and the whole of Emilia-Romagna has been combined with the other provinces of the Northeast to form one section. Shortly after the *Risorgimento* the Northeast was distinguished by the highest density of population in Italy and shared with the Northwest small community size, a high literacy rate, and a preference for the political Right.

Tuscany. Customarily classified as part of Central Italy, this region warrants separate treatment. Ethnic individuality is given the region by the Etruscans who settled there. Arriving from Asia Minor later than other early races and possessing great metallurgical skills, they dominated this and adjoining regions for hundreds of years and even Rome for a time. Furthermore, Tuscany was not included in the Papal States as were the other central provinces; nor was it as actively occupied by Austria as were the provinces in the Northeast. Rather it was a separate entity for more than three hundred years, suffering Austrian princelings on the throne and paying tax tributes to Vienna. In community size and a very strong preference for the political Right, Tuscany and its people displayed clear individuality. In ability to read they were very close to the national average; but in their linguistic tradition, captured by Dante and made the standard of modern Italian, they exhibited strong sectional identity.

East Central. Peopled early by Villanovans from the North, its modern status is importantly influenced by six hundred years of Papal rule. The States of the Church comprised the general areas of the modern provinces of Umbria, Marche, and Lazio. With the exception of Romagna, already noted, the small state of San Marino, and some minor boundary adjustments, this Central region possesses the least ambiguous political background of all Italy. A low density of population for Mainland Italy, less than average education, large communities, and a preference for the Right characterize this section. Moreover, an exhaustive supervision of local affairs by the Papacy, through organizations such as the *Buon Governo,* [9] gave a definite character and administrative unity to this section.

By combining diversified areas, the usual division of Italy into North,

9. A notable bureaucratic organ of the Church effective in promoting the financial and political organization of the Papal States and cultivating the growing spirit of nationalism.

Central, South, and Insular tends to obscure essential differences. The political preference of Sardinia for the Right and the lower literacy of its people are obliterated by the larger population of Sicily when Sicily and Sardinia are combined in an Insular region. Likewise, special features of literacy, population density, and community size are only a few of the salient variations lost to sight in the East Central section when it is averaged with dissimilar Tuscany to produce the conventional Central Italy.[10] There is danger, of course, in carrying a subdivision of this sort too far, for it is always possible to find intriguing differences which demand still further subdivision. The seven units suggested here are marginally justified, however. Although they increase the number of sections by three, this increased cost in time is compensated for by a greater return in the form of a more logical and historically valid division of the country for social study.

This, however, is only a first step in attacking the problem of regional development. A second and related step is necessary if full use is to be made of the available information. Although the numerical evidence from Italy's past is voluminous, it is available in different forms. Much of it appears in summaries which apply to the country as a whole; examples are national income figures, cost-of-living indexes, and trade statistics. Much less of the material is assembled into regional totals useful in a study of this kind; typically available at this level are population, housing, and election series. Finally, a great deal of it is found only in raw form at the provincial and community levels. In the use of such local information available in archives, community records, and other discrete sources, a sampling is helpful. Thereby, this wealth of data may be employed without the danger of its becoming enmeshed in a welter of detail.

10. Values computed from the same sources and corresponding to those shown in Table 1 for the normal division of Italy into North, Central, South, and Insular are as follows:

	North	Central	South	Insular	Italy
Density of population, average number of persons per square mile, 1871	303	208	218	156	234
Size of community, average area in square miles, 1871	8	23	18	28	14
Reading ability, per cent of persons age 6 and over able to read, 1871	46	28	17	15	31
Political preference, per cent of vote for Right party, 1874	70	74	33	23	54

A sample of provinces

Italy is divided into 19 districts, 91 provinces, and 7,871 communities.[11] For sampling purposes, the districts are too large and inclusive, while the communities are too subordinate and diverse to serve adequately the purpose of general economic analysis. Provinces alone are both numerous enough to offer ample choice and inclusive enough to provide a workable cross-section of statistical information.

Stratified sampling was used in selecting provinces which parallel the regions. Because of the small number involved and the possibility of simplifying the analysis by choosing similar provinces, a random sample was not employed. Instead, a kind of *ceteris paribus* technique was utilized, in which similar provinces were chosen from each of the seven regions of Italy. Important variables, topography and population density, were held roughly constant from province to province in order to facilitate observation of differences in economic institutions. Provinces containing large administrative centers were avoided so as to minimize the special problems associated with large regional capitals. Again, attention was given to the historical development of areas to insure that the tradition of the selected province was typical of the region as a whole. Applying these criteria, for which reliable statistics are available, to the ninety-one provinces conserved scarce economic time series and yielded seven provinces broadly similar in appearance and generally representative of the sections from which they were chosen.

Beyond the immediate motive of drawing this sample there is a broader goal in following these steps in detail, i.e., the uncovering of some additional dimensions of the country and its regions. Each of the stages in selecting individual provinces tells something of the scope of internal differences and their geographic arrangement. Thus, a better perspective is gained of the range of variables on which national and regional averages are based.

Convenience rather than importance dictated the actual sequence of steps. In accordance with this procedure, the patently redundant provinces could be discarded before time had been spent on them to establish a precise preferential ranking. The data and discussion in the first

---

11. A. Bruno, *Nuovo dizionario dei comuni e frazioni di comuni* (Rome: Tipografico Fausto Failli, 1954), p. 271; or for this general organization see tables in almost any of the publications of the Central Statistical Institute which follow the classification prescribed by the Constitution, approved December 22, 1947.

six steps exclude Sardinia; basic differences in provincial organization, population density, and range of selection justify treating this island separately from the more homogeneous Mainland Italy and Sicily.

Special home rule. Local government privileges are enjoyed by the peripheral regions of Italy, Valley of Aosta, Trentino-Alto Adige, Friuli-Venezia Giulia, Sicily, and Sardinia. Semi-autonomy was granted these areas because they have come under Italian control recently, or otherwise possess political and social characteristics which differ from surrounding sections. Accordingly the Valley of Aosta and four provinces in Northern Italy were discarded, for a sufficient representation of independent regimes is available already in Sicily and Sardinia. Further representation of these five decentralized regions would be *de trop*.[12]

Administrative centers. Chief towns of regions and the capitals of earlier royal administrations were avoided. Urbanization creates special problems and solutions atypical of the country as a whole,[13] and proximity to higher authority tends to influence local administrations. Thus, the people of Naples were accorded tax privileges at the expense of the rural subjects of Charles III. The avoidance of major cities is especially pertinent in Italy, where much of the literature and statistics is concerned with urban centers unrepresentative of the country as a whole. Consequently seventeen additional provinces were eliminated because they contained centers of administrative importance.[14]

New and altered provinces. To measure historical change requires political units of some antiquity and territorial continuity. With the *Risorgimento* a thoroughgoing revision of existing provincial boundaries took place, and under Fascist auspices in 1927 a large-scale creation of new provinces occurred. In addition, national treaties have brought about territorial modifications and resultant provincial changes. Many boundaries have been altered and more than a score of new provinces have been created since 1870. In consideration of these

12. Provinces excluded were Bolzano, Trento, Udine, Gorizia, and Trieste. (The order of listing provinces follows the North-South, West-East system adopted by the Central Statistical Institute.)

13. Note stress laid on this facet by B. F. Hoselitz, "The Role of Cities in the Economic Growth of Underdeveloped Countries," *Journal of Political Economy*, LXI (1953), pp. 195–208.

14. Turin, Genoa, Milan, Venice, Bologna, Ancona, Florence, Perugia, Rome, Naples, Aquila, Bari, Potenza, Palermo, and Catania; and, both Catanzaro and Reggio Calabria because the administrative offices in the Calabria region are divided between these two centers.

shifts, twenty-eight other provinces that had been largely modified in area or newly created since 1870 were discarded.[15]

Population density. A high density of population characterizes most parts of Italy except Sardinia. In 1871 on the Mainland and in Sicily the density was 249 persons for each square mile, ranging rather narrowly from a high of 280 in the Northeast to a low of 191 in the East Central section. Consistent with the goal of maintaining a relatively uniform density of population among the sample provinces, twenty-two provinces with densities deviating from the average of Mainland Italy and Sicily by more than 15 per cent were discarded.[16]

Topography. Except for the area along the Po River, a rugged, mixed terrain influences the economy of most parts of the country. The Alps, the Apennines, and their foothills extend over such a wide area that communications, soil cultivation, irrigation, and other topographical problems associated with mountains and hills are important in each of the nineteen administrative regions. On the other hand, problems connected with plains are much less serious in most areas and totally lacking in many, especially in Central Italy. Examined broadly, Italy is almost everywhere a mixture of mountains, hills, and plains. It is thus reasonable to discard as atypical Imperia, Avellino, and Campobasso with no plains (Table 2), since Cuneo and Salerno remain to represent these regions more adequately. At the same time, both Macerata and Ascoli Piceno need to be retained since no more typical provinces are available from the East Central area. In partial dispensation for this rejection of the one and acceptance of the other is the fact that the area does engross only 10 per cent of plains *in toto*. A similar situation prevails in Rovigo, Ferrara, Pisa, and Trapani where no

15. Ministero di Agricoltura, Industria e Commercio, Ufficio Centrale di Statistica, *Popolazione presente ed assente per comuni centri e frazioni di comune, Censimento 31 decembre 1871* (Rome: Stamperia Reale, 1874), I, Parte seconda, pp. 303–5; and SVIMEZ, *op. cit.*, pp. 1007–21. Of the remaining provinces those rejected because of newness or changes are: Vercelli, Novara, Asti, Alessandria, Savona, La Spezia, Varese, Como, Mantova, Massa-Carrara, Pistoia, Leghorn, Terni, Viterbo, Rieti, Latina, Frosinone, Caserta, Teramo, Pescara, Taranto, Brindisi, Lecce, Matera, Caltanissetta, Enna, Ragusa, and Syracuse.

16. These provinces and their population densities in persons per square mile are: Sondrio (90), Bergamo (346), Parma (392), Cremona (443), Mantova (469), Verona (307), Vicenza (346), Belluno (124), Treviso (369), Padova (441), Ravenna (308), Forli (208), Pesaro and Urbino (191), Lucca (410), Arezzo (188), Siena (140), Grosseto (62), Benevento (292), Chieti (340), Foggia (116), Cosenza (171), and Messina (335). Densities of population computed from Ministero dell'Interno, Direzione Generale di Statistica, *Annario statistico italiano: 1874* (Rome: Tipografia Elzeviriana, 1878), Parte prima, pp. 30–31; Istituto Centrale di Statistica, *Annuario statistico italiano: 1962* (Rome: Istituto Poligrafico dello Stato, 1963), pp. 2–3; and SVIMEZ, *op. cit.*, pp. 1007–21.

mountains exist. However, in this case Pisa must be retained since no more representative province exists from the Tuscan scene. Therefore, after a comparison of the proportions of mountains, hills, and plains in the remaining provinces with the proportions in the sections they were to represent, six additional provinces were discarded.[17]

Table 2. *Percentage distribution of the topography of certain provinces and section of Italy*

	Mountains	Hills	Plains	Total
Italy (less Sardinia)	37	39	24	100
Northwest	52	28	20	100
Cuneo	51	27	22	100
Imperia*	59	41	0	100
Northeast	44	15	41	100
Brescia	56	16	28	100
Rovigo*	0	0	100	100
Piacenza	36	37	27	100
Parma	43	32	25	100
Reggio Emilia	32	24	44	100
Modena	35	17	48	100
Ferrara*	0	0	100	100
Tuscany	25	66	9	100
Pisa	0	74	26	100
East Central	28	62	10	100
Macerata	32	68	0	100
Ascoli Piceno	26	74	0	100
South	35	45	20	100
Avellino*	68	32	0	100
Salerno	29	60	11	100
Campobasso*	55	45	0	100
Sicily	25	61	14	100
Trapani*	0	51	49	100
Agrigento	13	72	15	100

*Provinces eliminated because of nontypical topography.
Source: Computed from Istituto Centrale di Statistica, *Annuario statistico italiano: 1962* (Rome: Istituto Poligrafico dello Stato, 1963), pp. 2–3. June 30, 1961, data used because earlier statistics contained only a simple dichotomy, mountains and plains, for example. *Annuario statistico italiano: 1878*, Parte prima, pp. II-V.

Historical background. No further screening was applied where only single provinces within an area survived the first five tests. In the Northeast and East Central sections, however, where more than one province still remained and where exact sectional boundaries are fluid, final selection was based on the capacity of each province to represent

17. Imperia, Rovigo, Ferrara, Avellino, Campobasso, and Trapani.

the economic tradition of the region. Among Brescia, Piacenza, Parma, Reggio Emilia, and Modena, the first is definitely to be selected; the last four provinces, although under Austrian domination for a long period, were in the Emilia-Romagna region and thus subject to a degree of control more comparable with Tuscany's than with the active occupation experienced by Brescia and the whole of Lombardy. Between Macerata and Ascoli Piceno there is little to choose. Both are located in regions without plains; both lie well within the area dominated by the ancient Picenes; and both now have economies of mixed industry and agriculture. Although Ascoli Piceno rests almost on the border between the East Central and Southern regions, and was held momentarily by the Kingdom of Naples, it was chosen over Macerata because, by such measures as a lower rate of migration,[18] it displays better the remote and independent character of much of Marche, Umbria, and Lazio.

Sardinia. Because this island is quite different from mainland Italy and Sicily, the selection of a representative province requires the breaking of almost all the criteria used in choosing the other sample provinces. A Carthaginian stronghold for years, it is still remote from national influences. Of the three provinces now on Sardinia, Nuoro was created in 1927 and must be discarded on the practical ground of possessing too brief a history. Cagliari's topography is confined to hills and plains and is, therefore, not typical of the mixed terrain of the island. The third province, Sassari, is the most usable; it not only has a great antiquity, but also a configuration and population density reasonably close to the average for all of Sardinia.[19]

Thus, the final sample comprises: *Northwest*—Cuneo, *Northeast*—Brescia, *Tuscany*—Pisa, *East Central*—Ascoli Piceno, *South*—Salerno, *Sicily*—Agrigento, and *Sardinia*—Sassari. With the exception of Sassari,

18. Compare two booklets, Direzione Generale della Statistica, *Annali di Statistica: Fascicolo 41, Notizie sulle condizioni industriali della provincia di Ascoli Piceno,* and *Fascicolo 42, Notizie sulle condizioni industriali della provincia di Macerata* (Rome: Tipografia Nazionale di G. Bertero, 1892), p. 6 in each.

19. Density and terrain figures are as follows:

	Population density (persons per square mile)	Percentage of land in		
		Mountains	Hills	Plains
Sardinia	68	14	68	18
Sassari	84	11	74	15

Source: Annuario statistico italiano: 1878, Parte prima, p. 31; *1962,* p. 3; and SVIMEZ, *op. cit.,* p. 1020.

all of the provinces were generally similar in population density and land topography to Italy as a whole in 1871. Each province was firmly entrenched in the economic heritage of its region. And none was subject to the special problems or traditions of urban centers. In short, at the time of Unification, though possessing backgrounds common to the larger sections, these provinces were roughly equal in the cardinal features of the Italian environment.

Change in region and province

Comparing economic change is a useful device for assessing the scope of the problem of national unity. It is also a helpful method for testing the utility of the sample. Five statistical measures derived from meticulous official reports provide authentic material for these purposes. Before looking more specifically at the individual regions, it is possible to extract from them some indication of the way sectional forces established in the past have matured and to gain some preliminary notion of the magnitude of the forces in question.

Alterations in population density are of paramount importance in shaping the whole economy and each of its parts. Increases in the number of readers in the population and extensions in the road system are rough indicators of the accomplishments of public expenditures in areas of primary consequence: education and public works. Shifts in political preference, as voters move away from the Center parties toward the Left and the Right, give measurable indication of the citizen's reactions to his environment. And dependence of workers on agriculture for employment reflects the transforming focus of industrial activity and general economic change.

Sectional variations in economic activity since Unification should be illuminated by this sample. Over almost a century the major regions of Italy have responded in different ways to economic change. If this sample is usable, these regional alterations should be reflected in comparable shifts in the sample provinces. Possibly, also, the other movements discernible only at this level may add refinements to the economic profile of the section and the nation.

No special adjustments have been made for changes in the size of administrative areas. Only small modifications in territory occurred as boundaries were refined and new provinces created. Apart from some trivial bias introduced by concentrations on the older, more fully established provinces, the problem of changes in territory is easily overcome. Since the provinces themselves are samples of larger sections, variations in the area are essentially unimportant fluctuations in the size of the sample. Thus, interpretation of statistical movements from them requires only an awareness of the magnitude of the change for possible variations in economies of scale and the appropriate statement of the results on a per person or other applicable per unit basis.

Change in density of population. In ninety years the population of the nation increased in a sectional pattern on an average of 195 persons per square mile (Table 3). Large advances in the East Central, South, and Sicily regions contrast with the relatively smaller ones in the Northwest, Northeast, Tuscany, and, especially, Sardinia. The different population developments reflect varied reproduction rates, internal and foreign migrations, and a strong tendency toward urbanization. In the East Central section the creation of the national capital tended to inflate the average growth in this area far beyond that of the nation as a whole. Among the sample provinces, Cuneo and Salerno show extremes of density change, as rural areas of the Northwest lost population and the urban centers of the South gained in a general movement from villages to the greater economic opportunities of city life.

Change in the public sphere. Government activity produced substantial gains. Measured by the tangible evidence of the number of adults who could read and the extensiveness of the road network, advances were recorded in every region. The 1871 sectional pattern of higher literacy in the North than in the South persisted, but was being reduced in most sections at least as late as 1961, the last year in which information was published in such detail. With only one contrasting exception, changes among the sample provinces were broadly similar to those occurring in their respective regions. In Brescia, substantial, although well below average, gains were achieved from a very high level of literacy in 1871. Based on advances in literacy, the results of Italian Unification are both widely evident and keenly felt.

Modern requirements that roads bear motor traffic make precise historical comparisons unreliable. It is true that ancient Roman roads, with a light surfacing of asphalt, still carry heavy vehicle traffic, but these are the exception. It is possible to say only that the length of

Table 3. *Changes in certain social measures occurring in Italy and her parts since Unification*

				Regions of Italy				
Characteristic, Unit, Period	North-west	North-east	Tuscany	East Central	South	Sicily	Sardinia	
				Sample provinces				
	Cuneo	Brescia	Pisa	Ascoli Piceno	Salerno	Agri-gento	Sassari	Italy
Population density, change in average number of persons per square mile, 1871 to 1961								
Regions	162	190	140	255	206	239	80	195
Provinces	−25	194	162	155	213	187	45	
Reading ability, change in average number of readers per 100 persons aged 6 and over, 1871 to 1961								
Regions	43	55	61	68	67	69	72	60
Provinces	48	42	62	71	68	69	71	
Road mileage, change in average number of feet of roads per square mile of territory, 1876 to 1962								
Regions	3766	3189	3150	3455	3015	2710	1263	3230
Provinces	2901	−306	2558	5570	2685	2174	1451	
Political preference, change in average number of voters in every 100 supporting Center parties in elections for Chamber of Deputies, 1948 to 1963								
Regions	−5	−5	−6	−12	−9	−9	−6	−8
Provinces	0	−5	−4	−17	−3	−10	−16	
Agricultural dependence, change in average number of men in each 100 engaged in farming, hunting, or fishing, 1871 to 1961								
Regions	−42	−38	−33	−37	−28	−19	−36	−34
Provinces	−25	−41	−29	−30	−30	−20	−34	

Source: Population figures—*Censimento 31 dicembre 1871*, I, Parte seconda, pp. 303–5, *Annuario statistico italiano: 1878*, Parte prima, pp. 30–31; *1965*, pp. 2–3 and 10–11. Literacy data—*Censimento 31 dicembre 1871*, II, pp. B, C, F, G, H, and L; and *10° Censimento generale della popolazione, 15 novembre 1961*, III, pp. 24–27; IV, pp. 597–605, 782–97; and V, pp. 136–39. Road information—*Annuario statistico italiano: 1878*, Parte prima, pp. 30–31, and Supplemento, pp. 2–3 and 244–45. Election results—Istituto Centrale di Statistica and Ministero dell'Interno, *Le elezioni politiche del 1948, Elezione della Camera dei Deputati* (Rome: Fausto Failli, 1951), I, pp. 128–33 and 144; and Istituto Centrale di Statistica and Ministero dell'Interno, *Elezione della Camera dei Deputati, 28 aprile 1963* (Rome: Istituto Poligrafico dello Stato, 1965), I, pp. 18–49; and Istituto Centrale di Statistica and Ministero dell'Interno, *Elezioni della Camera dei Deputati e del Senato della Repubblica, Dati riassuntivi* (Rome: Istituto Poligrafico dello Stato, 1963), pp. 32–33. Occupational details— *Censimento 31 dicembre 1871*, III, pp. lxviii–lxix, 12, 26, 27, 28, 29, 94, 96, 111, 113, 131, and 133; and *10° Censimento generale della popolazione, 15 ottobre 1961*, III, Appendice, pp. 28–31. For occupational details the 1871 figures include men aged fifteen and over; those for 1961 include men aged ten and over.

roads has more than doubled in eighty-odd years. The national survey figures used in Table 3, however, imply an intensified pattern of improvement in which the more extensive road systems in Northern and Central regions were expanded more fully than were the more primitive systems of the South, Sicily, and, especially, Sardinia.

Provincial figures behave somewhat differently from sectional ones. Construction and maintenance of streets and highways is one of the largest civic expenses under communal jurisdiction.[20] Thus, the extensive development in Ascoli Piceno measures a local vitality and progressiveness from the low level of 1876 to an extremely high one in 1962. Contrasted with this the Brescia figure represents a more conservative implementation of a road system already large in 1876.

Change in the political sphere.[21] Since World War II the general elections for the Chamber of Deputies have shown a pronounced shift away from the Center parties. There has been some movement to the Right, but more to the Left, and just recently toward a Center-Left coalition.[22] Nationally, the strong 61 per cent majority of the Center was reduced to 53 per cent and "an opening to the Left." Locally,

20. Roughly one fifth of the highway system is classified as national and two fifths each as provincial and communal. These figures do not include city streets under communal jurisdiction. *Annuario di statistiche provinciali: 1963*, pp. 244–45; and *Annuario statistico italiano: 1965*, p. 289.

21. Extremely helpful in preparing this section was Joseph G. La Palombara, "The Italian Elections and the Problem of Representation," *American Political Science Review*, XLVII (1953), pp. 676–703.

22. Classification of principal parties in these elections is as follows:

1948	*1963*
Center	
Christian Democrat (Democrazia Cristiana)	Christian Democrat (Democrazia Cristiana)
United Socialist (Unità Socialista)	Democratic Socialist (Partito Socialista Democratico Italiano)
National Bloc (Blocco Nazionale)	Liberal (Partito Liberale Italiano)
Republican (Partito Repubblicano Italiano)	Republican (Partito Repubblicano Italiano)
Left	
Democratic Front (Fronte Democratico Popolare per la Libertà, la Pace, il Lavoro)	Socialist (Partito Socialista Italiano)
	Communist (Partito Communista Italiano)
Right	
National Monarchist and Democratic Labor Alliance (Partito Nazionale Monarchico e Alleanza Democratica Nazionale del Lavoro)	United Monarchy (Partito Democratico Italiano di Unità Monarchica)
Social Movement (Movimento Sociale Italiano)	Social Movement (Movimento Sociale Italiano)

these losses were spread widely in each of the regions and in all but one of the sample provinces. Counterbalancing shifts were recorded by both the Right and the Left. Increases and then decreases by the Right, especially in the East Central, South, and Insular regions, were contrasted by progressive growth in the Left. In sum, losses by the Center parties between 1948 and 1963, as shown in Table 3, can be viewed as gains by the Left.

Sectionally, the change was important because it gave the Left a clear majority of the seats in Tuscany. Provincially, political concentration tends to aggregate in areas outside of the more cosmopolitan urban centers. In Cuneo the Center, in Salerno the Right, and in Pisa the Left hold substantially larger concentrations than the regions they represent. In all sections—particularly in the East Central, South, Sicily, and Sardinia—continued losses by the Center and more recently by the Right have contributed to the success of the Left. This, in turn, has led to the advent of a Center-Left coalition divorced from the Communists but reinforced by the fusion of the Socialists. These alterations might almost be interpreted as a recurrence of dissatisfaction with the prevailing order and a demand for a shift to a more forceful administration of regional problems.

Change in the economic sphere. As measured by a decline in dependence on agriculture for employment, economic gains also followed a sectional pattern. Between 1871 and 1961, the most recent year for which figures in this detail are presently available, a full one third of the nation's males moved from the primary occupations of farming, hunting, and fishing to other employment. Industrialization, especially in the Northwest and the Northeast, accounts for much of this shift. Except in the Northwest, differences in experience between region and province have not been large. The notable inference is that all areas shared in the economic miracle of Italian development.[23] Actually, in the South and Sicily the change in occupations over the years was less impressive than in the North. Again, Sardinia behaved quite differently from other Southern and Insular regions. With these exceptions, the flow of men from these primary activities was large, and more a Northern than a Southern phenomenon.

Apparently much the same sectional pattern of development took

23. See details of the Italian miracle in George H. Hildebrand, *Growth and Structure in the Economy of Modern Italy* (Cambridge: Harvard University Press, 1965), pp. 3–104.

place in other statistical series. Thus, the gulfs between parts of the
country are not confined to the few topics noted here, but extend to
the whole field of social evidence. For example, even the ethnological
measure of the heights of men called for military service, reflecting in
part the economic factors of available nutritional and health facilities,
follows a sectional pattern. Greater improvements were recorded in the
already generally taller statures of those from the Northwest, Northeast,
Tuscany, and the East Central sections, while smaller growths were realized by those from the South, Sicily, and the Sardinia areas. Application
of the t-test to the published frequency distributions shows the im-
probability that these differences could have occurred by chance.[24]

Even at this initial level profound internal variations suggest themselves. Political unification—the realized goal of the triumvirate, Cavour,
Mazzini, and Garibaldi, as well as of millions of other Italians—seems
not to have resulted in economic unity. It is true, of course, that custom
duties are levied at the national border and internal taxes are largely
dictated from Rome. But, more fundamentally, population groups still
exhibit substantial differences in economic wellbeing.

With the regions of the country outlined and the sample provinces
designated, it is possible to fill out the characteristics of each of these
component parts of Italy in terms of income. Viewed as a whole, Italy
has achieved better living standards since the *Risorgimento*. Examined
internally by region and by province, the advance has not been uniform.
In fact, as noted in the next chapter, improvements in cities are not
matched by comparable progress in rural areas; and better conditions in
Northern sections are not approached by Southern gains. Growing urbanization and sectionalism, the net result of a complex matrix of historical forces, exemplify a continuing differentiation in Italy. Perhaps
the benefits of Italian unity have not been shared universally.

24. *Annuario statistico italiano:* 1878, Parte prima, pp. 72–75; and *1962*, p. 58. For a
detailed study see: Alessandro Costanzo, "La statura degli italiani ventenni nati dal
1854 al 1920," *Annali di Statistica*, Series 8, II (1948).

3. *Recent growth and status*

> *But neither the median forests, how rich soever their land,*
> *Neither Ganges the lovely, nor Hermus cloudy with golden*
>   *sand,*
> *With Italy's glories may vie. . . .*
> — Vergil (trans. A. S. Way)

The economy as a whole

Several measures reflect the expanding capacity of the Italian economy during the recent past of statistical literacy. Notable is the national income series dating from 1860. Stated in real per capita terms, these figures show Italy traversing three broad stages since then. The first starts with Garibaldi's march and ends with the turn of the century. Although final unification was achieved, it produced little immediate improvement in economic conditions. Apart from minor fluctuations, real per capita income remained virtually unchanged for thirty years (Chart 1). The second stage begins in 1900 and continues until World War II. In spite of the setback occasioned by the "last war of the *Risorgimento*" from 1915 to 1918, the onslaught of Fascism in 1922, and the depression of the 1930's, income increased at a surprisingly persistent rate of slightly more than 1 per cent each year. And the third stage includes the years between the ending of World War II and the present. During this time, encouraged by foreign assistance and the Common Market, a growth rate of almost 5 per cent per year has been maintained.

As a result of this growth, per capita income in Italy has trebled in this century. In lire of 1960 purchasing power, it increased from less than 120,000 in 1860 to almost 400,000 by 1960.[1] This means that Italy's income ranks roughly midway among the fifty-five nations of the world submitting suitable evidence to the Statistical Office of the United Nations.[2] Tenuous as national comparisons of income are, they do re-

1. Istituto Centrale di Statistica, *Sommario di statistiche storiche italiane: 1861–1955* (Rome: Istituto Poligrafico dello Stato, 1958), p. 216.
2. Statistical Office of the United Nations, *Per Capita National Product of Fifty-five Countries: 1952–1954* (New York: United Nations, 1957), p. 7.

Chart 1. *Net national product per capita for Italy, constant lire (1960)*

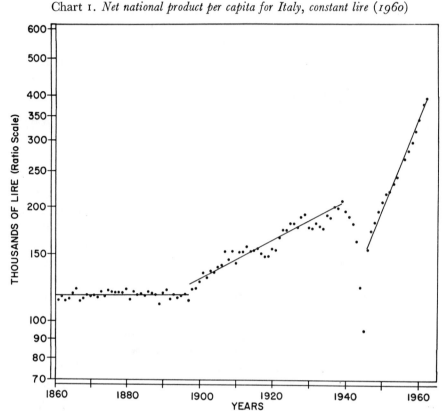

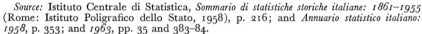

Source: Istituto Centrale di Statistica, *Sommario di statistiche storiche italiane: 1861–1955*
(Rome: Istituto Poligrafico dello Stato, 1958), p. 216; and *Annuario statistico italiano:
1958*, p. 353; and *1963*, pp. 35 and 383–84.

veal in broad terms something of the panorama of income levels. With
Italy at a height of slightly over three hundred, measured in U.S. dollars
per person in 1952–54, the others range from Uganda and Burma with
fifty each to the United States with nineteen hundred. Looking at the
narrower area of Western Europe, Italy's per capita income in 1955
was about one-half that of the leaders—Denmark, the United Kingdom,
Norway, and Belgium.[3] This represented a substantial improvement of
its relative position in 1950, because among the nations of Western

3. Milton Gilbert and Associates, *Comparative National Products and Price Levels* (Paris:
Organization for European Economic Cooperation, 1958), p. 23.

Europe its rate of growth in per capita income during these five years was exceeded only by West Germany.

Internationally, these Italian gains are very impressive. Domestically, behind the façade of national averages, there is not a void but a number of both real and apparent improvements. They may be considered first in terms of the economic sectors of the economy and then on the basis of its regional structure.

In back of the improvements in per capita income there have been a number of advances and declines in activities on which this income is based. A helpful measure of one critical sector is the index of industrial production shown in Table 4. It indicates that production in this area has almost quadrupled in the post-World War II period. Based on the production of mines, manufacturing establishments, power plants, and gas producers, it shows a rapidly expanding economy. In fact, when these figures are plotted they reveal an exponential series that is growing more rapidly even than the income figures in the sharply sloping section of Chart 1. Where the income data record 5 per cent per annum, the industrial production index displays almost 7 per cent.

Table 4. *Index of Italian industrial production* (1958 = 100)

Year	Index	Year	Index
1938	43		
		1955	84
1948	44	1956	90
1949	48	1957	96
1950	56	1958	100
1951	62	1959	111
1952	64	1960	128
1953	70	1961	142
1954	76	1962	156

Source: Derived from Statistical Office of the United Nations, *Statistical Yearbook: 1957* (New York: United Nations, 1957), p. 135; and *1963*, p. 100.

Apparent, too, are the steps in this interest-like growth which feeds on its previous gains. By 1948 its level had equalled and bettered the 1938, prewar figure; by 1956 it had doubled it, and by 1960 it was a full three times as large. The firms represented in this index which were producing chemicals, automobiles and trucks, petroleum products, plastics, and artificial fibers were among those registering the greatest gains. The advances shown in Table 4 are especially noteworthy, for since 1938 the index has not included the construction industry which had perhaps the most spectacular growth of all components of the economy.

A more perceptive understanding of this phenomenon of growth and the role of industrial production and construction in it can be had from an examination of another time series. This one states in systematic fashion the behavior of the major sectors of the economy in recent years. Presented in Table 5 it shows the way the sectors contributing to Italy's gross domestic product have changed in recent years. In effect it illustrates how some parts of the economy have grown, others have remained virtually the same, and still others have declined in relative importance since 1938.

Table 5. *Percentage distribution of the industrial origin of the Italian gross domestic product at factor cost for 1938 and 1947–1963, inclusive*

Year	Agriculture, forestry, fishing	Mining	Manufacturing	Construction	Transportation and communications	Trade and commerce	Public administration and defense	All others	Total
1938	27	1	25	2	9	13	11	12	100
1947	38	1	29	2	6	11	6	7	100
1948	36	1	28	3	6	10	8	8	100
1949	31	1	30	2	6	10	10	10	100
1950	29	1	31	3	6	9	10	11	100
1951	27	1	31	3	6	9	10	13	100
1952	26	1	31	5	6	9	11	11	100
1953	26	1	31	5	6	9	10	12	100
1954	24	1	31	6	7	9	10	12	100
1955	23	1	31	6	7	9	10	13	100
1956	21	1	31	6	7	9	11	14	100
1957	20	1	31	7	7	9	11	14	100
1958	20	1	31	7	7	9	11	14	100
1959	19	1	31	7	7	9	11	15	100
1960	17	1	32	7	7	9	11	16	100
1961	18	1	33	7	7	9	11	14	100
1962	17	1	33	8	7	9	11	14	100
1963	16	1	33	8	7	9	12	14	100

Source: Adapted from *Statistical Yearbook, 1959*, p. 452; and *1964*, p. 152.

Four of the categories advanced. They were construction, manufacturing, government, and the "all others" heading which includes such subgroups as services and the ownership of dwellings. Growth was greatest in construction. In 1947 it represented 2 per cent of the gross domestic product; in 1963, it made up four times as much, or 8 per cent. For the growth of the economy as a whole this was of importance, especially in the early part of the period when much of it was devoted to enlarging plants and fabricating facilities in general. The continued relative improvement of manufacturing is possibly the single strongest feature in Italian postwar development. As early as 1950 it replaced agriculture as the largest sector in the economy.

In the public sphere as revealed by the category, "public administration and defense," there has also been a continued growth, to the extent that "all services of the general government" in 1963 made up twice as big a share of the total as they did in 1947. Contrasting these expansions are the primary activities of agriculture, forestry, and fishing which have declined notably in size. In brief, behind a rising per capita income there have been substantial alterations in the composition of the Italian economy. These changes are characterized by a rapid actual and relative expansion in industry, construction, and government, offset by a relative decline in agriculture. A question of moment is: Were these gains shared widely? From a nationwide point of view a partial answer to this question may be found in an examination of the concurrent changes in employment opportunities.

Table 6. *Recent status of the Italian labor force*

Year	Labor force (000,000)			Total resident population (000,000)	Unemployed as percentage of labor force	Labor force as percentage of total population
	Employed	Unemployed	Total			
1952	18.9	1.5	20.4	47.2	7	43
1954	19.2	1.7	20.9	47.9	8	44
1955	20.0	1.5	21.5	48.3	7	45
1956	19.7	1.9	21.6	48.7	9	44
1957	20.4	1.7	22.1	49.1	8	45
1958	21.1	1.3	22.4	49.6	6	45
1959	20.9	1.1	22.0	49.8	5	44
1960	20.9	0.8	21.7	50.3	4	43
1961	21.2	0.7	21.9	50.7	3	43
1962	21.0	0.6	21.6	51.2	3	42
1963	20.1	0.5	20.6	50.5	2	41
1964	20.0	0.6	20.6	51.2	3	40

Source: Developed from *Annuario statistico italiano: 1957*, p. 352; *1958*, p. 306; *1960*, p. 317; *1962*, p. 359; and *1965*, p. 353. In this and subsequent tables calculations are made prior to rounding and adjustments are made to preserve internal consistency.

Job opportunities did not show a relative improvement over the last decade and more. As indicated in Table 6, employment registered some fluctuating increase over the years between 1952 and 1964. These findings are based on a series of samples taken once each year during the earlier part of the period and at four spaced intervals in the latter part. In spite of some minor change in definitions, this is a record of persons fourteen years of age and over who were working or looking for work in the sample week, plus individuals temporarily working abroad, those working occasionally, and youngsters ten to fourteen years of age regularly employed.

The jobs these people held reached and slightly exceeded twenty-one million in several years, a gain of more than two million over the initial year, 1952. But this high level was not maintained, and the total of jobs dropped back to twenty million—an advance of only one million, one hundred thousand over the full term of years in Table 6. During this same time unemployment declined from a high level which ranged between one and one-half and almost two million in the early part of the period to a low of about one-half million at the end. In spite of these changes, the size of the labor force in 1964 was just about what it had been in 1952, roughly twenty and one-half million persons. It is true that these gainfully employed individuals grew in number to almost twenty-two and one-half million during the middle years, but they declined again at the end. Overall, then, during the years from 1952 to 1964 there was almost no change in the size of the labor force; within this number an increase in the number of jobs produced a corresponding decline in unemployment.

But during this same interval the total population grew by about four million persons. If the prevailing gainfully occupied rate of, say, 43 per cent of the population were maintained and no refinements were made for changes in the age-sex composition of the population, this would mean that the four million additional population might be expected to add one million, seven hundred thousand persons to the labor force. However, the labor force gained only about two hundred thousand persons between 1952 and 1964. This leaves roughly one and one-half million persons unaccounted for. If these people had entered the labor force as might have been expected, they might have swelled the unemployment lists to perhaps two million. But the labor force did not expand and unemployment did not grow. Instead, persons were encouraged to leave the labor market, or to refrain from entering it by such incentives as enlarged social security benefits, expanded aid to students, and increased efforts to keep women in the home. All of these discouragements to seeking employment were compounded by enlarged incomes which freed some members of the family from the need to work. If it had not been for these other factors functioning to reduce the relative size of the labor force, unemployment probably would have increased rather than decreased over the period, for clearly the employment expansion that did occur was not large enough to absorb the normal flow of persons from a growing population. Thus, increased incomes and shifts away from agriculture to industry, construction, and government actually resulted in not more, but relatively fewer jobs.

But all of these generalizations refer to the nation as a single geographic unit. As such, they conceal regional variations of vital moment in understanding these developments. A first step in looking beyond these national averages is an analysis of the way incomes in different parts of the country have changed. Statistics describing the geographic dispersion of income are, however, of recent origin and varied scope. Only in 1960 were official government figures of regional income published.[4] Dividing Italy into three sections the Central Institute of Statistics demarked an industrial Northwest, an agricultural Northeast, and a traditional South. Including not only the Piedmont, the Valley of Aosta, and Liguria, but also Lombardy as well, the first region is the industrial triangle of Italy. Embracing all the rest of Northern Italy down to and including Rome,[5] the second region, though traditionally agricultural in character, is being developed industrially by a series of public and semipublic corporations. And, following long usage, the Southern portion of the Italian Boot and the two islands of Sicily and Sardinia comprise the "South" of the Vanoni Plan and the Casa per il Mezzogiorno. Thus, individual responsibility and local initiative in the first region are offset against public partnership in the second and public aid in the third.

But attractive as this simple juxtaposition is, it is too pat a picture. The brush is too wide. This simple triplex in itself continues very broad averages involving dissimilar areas. It is true that substantial income differences exist among the three areas, but these are smaller than those revealed by a more scrupulous partition of the country. Furthermore,

---

4. Istituto Centrale di Statistica, "Primi studi sui conti economici territoriali," *Annali di Statistica*, Series 8, XII (1960).

5. *Ibid.*, pp. xii–xiii. In principle the district of Lazio is divided between the Northeast and the South. In practice, because of statistical difficulties concerning the figures referred to here, the Central Institute of Statistics has included all of it, even the provinces of Latina and Frosinone, in the Northeast.

growth rates of the three areas, also because of the effect of averaging, tend to be more narrowly ranged than the rates of their components.

The economy's constituent parts

Dividing Italy into seven regions makes feasible a greater delineation of the economic forces at work in the country. Varied rates of economic growth are shown. The centripetal and ameliorating pressures of urbanization are revealed. And, the consistent progress of advanced areas is contrasted with the pulsating evolution of depressed regions. In fact, several of the universal truths of economic development are exemplified in the statistical evidence made possible by the demarcation of Italy.

Compilation of detailed regional statistics of national income in Italy is largely the work of one man, Professor Guglielmo Tagliacarne. In a series of papers and articles he has made available estimates of income for the many sectors of Italy for 1938 and from 1951 through 1960.[6] Adapting official income statistics by use of indexes of wages, motor vehicle registration, power consumption, etc., he has developed provincial figures of income. Technically these estimates are the sum of the net product of the private sector and the net product of the public sector at factor cost. They are less than the usual concept of national income by the amount of net income from abroad. Since the figures for current net transfers from the rest of the world during these years do not bulk large in the total, they may be disregarded here. The estimates, then, may be referred to simply as the national income derived from each province.

An example of the composition of Italian national income in reference to other conventional product totals for the year 1960 is as follows:

6. Following a paper read before the Societa italiana di Statistica in Rome (January 8, 1953) concerning sectional income for 1951, Professor Tagliacarne prepared: "Calcolo del reddito del settore privato e della pubblica amministrazione nelle provincie e regioni d'Italia nel 1952," *Moneta e Credito*, VI (1953), pp. 149–91; under similar titles for the years 1953 and 1954, *Moneta e Credito*, VII (1954), pp. 165–212, and *Moneta e Credito*, VIII (1955), pp. 198–245, he presented data for these years. In 1955 he summarized his previous work in English, "Italy's Net National Product by Regions," *Banca Nazionale del Lavoro Review*, VIII (1955), pp. 215–31. In 1960 he revised his calculations for the years 1951 through 1959, first in "Anticipazioni sul calcolo del reddito prodotto nelle provincie e regioni d'Italia nel 1959 e confronti col 1958," *Moneta e Credito*, XIII (1960), pp. 385–89; and then more fully in "Calcolo del reddito prodotto dal settore privato e dalla pubblica amministrazione nelle provincie e regioni d'Italia nel 1959 e confronti con gli anni dal 1951 al 1959," *Moneta e Credito*, XIII (1960), pp. 439–551. Data from 1960 were added by him in "Calcolo del reddito prodotto dal settore privato e dalla pubblica amministrazione nelle provincie e regione d'Italia nel 1961 e confronto con gli anni 1960 e 1951," *Moneta e Credito*, XV (1962), pp. 339–419 and 513–34.

	Current lire[7] (000,000,000)
Gross National Product (GNP)	19,937
Less: Allowance for depreciation	1,881
Net National Product (NNP)	18,056
Less: Allowance for indirect taxes and subsidies	2,364
National Income (Net National Product at Factor Prices)	15,692
Less: Current transfers from abroad	76
Net Product of Private and Public Sectors	15,616

Actually, because of minor differences between the definitions employed by the United Nations and those used by the Central Institute of Statistics,[8] and because of upward revisions in the figures published earlier by the Institute,[9] the "Net Product of Private and Public Sectors" apportioned by Professor Tagliacarne is somewhat smaller than the one shown just above. In effect, he is concerned with the allocation among the provinces of a national income amounting to slightly less than fifteen trillion lire in 1960.[10]

Some estimates of provincial income for the years 1951 and 1952 were prepared also by Giovanni Cusimano.[11] In general they differ very little from those of Tagliacarne. In comparison with the three-region figures of the Central Institute of Statistics, both Cusimano's and Tagliacarne's distributions tend to be somewhat greater than official estimates.[12] In spite of shortcomings in all these data, each of the three series does mirror more or less precisely the rate of economic development in the diverse sections of Italy. The Tagliacarne estimates are particularly valuable since they have been prepared in detail over more than a decade.

Ideally, a measure of the growing capacity of plants and equipment, know-how and technology, raw materials and services, and labor and management is wanted. Instead there is an indication of the flow of goods and services through the market place. However, even if the ideal were realized, it would not be the perfect answer to a complete ap-

7. Statistical Office of the United Nations, *Yearbook of National Accounts Statistics: 1962* (New York: United Nations, 1963), p. 138.
8. Istituto Centrale di Statistica, "Indagine statistica sullo sviluppo del reddito nazionale dell'Italia dal 1861 al 1956," *Annali di Statistica,* Series 8, IX (1957), pp. 7–50.
9. Compare *Annuario statistico italiano: 1960,* pp. 355–59, with *Annuario statistico italiano: 1961,* pp. 371–76.
10. Tagliacarne, "Calcolo del reddito . . . anni 1960 e 1951," pp. 414–19.
11. Giovanni Cusimano, "Di alcuni criteri metodologici per la ripartizione del reddito nazionale fra le regioni d'Italia," *Rivista italiana di economia demografia e statistica,* VIII (1954), pp. 58–104.
12. "Primi studi sui conti economici territoriali." This theme is developed in Tagliacarne, "Calcolo del reddito . . . nel 1959 e . . . 1958," pp. 440–41.

praisal of economic growth; for conventionally, economic growth over-
looks any direct consideration of such items as increased leisure time,
advanced cultural development, and furthered knowledge beyond mar-
ketable skills.[13]

To increase a nation's rate of economic growth by even tenths of a
per cent per year is notoriously formidable.[14] It is true that growth
rates do fluctuate, sometimes widely, but to increase the slope of the
base line around which these variations occur is another matter. For
this reason, even small differences in rates of growth warrant careful
consideration and analysis. Two other arguments are pertinent. Concerning other parts of the world it is reasoned that the less developed
areas have a distinct statistical advantage over more developed regions
in the numbers game of economic growth. The less the development,
the lower the base, and so the more impressive the numerical increase.
Also, shifting production from home to factory during the early stages
of development brings goods into the market where they are counted
for the first time.[15] In Italy both of these phenomena influence the
figures. Therefore, small differences are intriguing, both because of the
stickiness of the rates and because of statistical bonanzas to the less developed areas.

The regional figures

In gross terms, national income almost doubled in Italy during the
1950's. Specifically, between the year 1951 and the year 1960 it increased by about 93 per cent (Table 7). More pertinent for this inquiry
is the behavior of the seven regions of the country. Three of them
equaled or bettered this national average. The East Central, including
Rome and its rapidly expanding environs, experienced the largest
growth. Next was Tuscany, and only just equal to the national average
was the Northeast of Milan and Venice.

Each of the other three sections showed less than average progress.
The Northeast, of course, was very close to the national average and
because of its high starting level achieved a really substantial improve-

13. Jean Fourastie refers to this complex as "le niveau de vie," in *Machinisme et Bien-
Être* (Paris: Editions de Minuit, 1951), pp. 16–19, and the translator, Theodore Caplow,
uses "style of life" in *The Causes of Wealth* (Glencoe, Illinois: Free Press, 1960), pp. 17–18.
14. Denison, *op. cit.*, pp. 5–7.
15. See an elaboration of these and other related points in Calvin B. Hoover, "National
Policy and the Rates of Economic Growth: The United States, Soviet Russia, and Western
Europe," *South Atlantic Quarterly*, LIX (1960), p. 480.

ment. Sicily, with a much lower initial level, recorded almost as high a rate as the Northwest. Only the South and Sardinia netted substantially smaller gains than the others. In gross terms, then, the East Central region stands alone; the Northwest, the Northeast, Tuscany, and Sicily form a predominant middle group; and the South and Sardinia advance at a distinctly lower rate.

Table 7. *Changes in the total income of the regions of Italy between 1951 and 1960*

Region	Total income, current lire (000,000,000)		Percentage change 1951 to 1960
	1951	*1960*	
Northwest	1,271	2,408	89
Northeast	3,174	6,110	93
Tuscany	499	970	94
East Central	820	1,835	124
South	1,224	2,191	79
Sicily	448	843	88
Sardinia	165	288	75
Italy	7,601	14,645	93

Source: Guglielmo Tagliacarne, "Calcolo del reddito prodotto dal settore privato e dalla pubblica amministrazione nelle provincie e regioni d'Italia nel 1961 e confronto con gli anni 1960 e 1951," *Moneta e Credito*, XV (1962), pp. 520–25.

These figures are of gross regional income, however, and so neglect the crucial variable of population. A region's income may expand impressively, but if it grows no faster than its population, the individual resident stands to gain no improvement in living standard. Since population increase is such a ubiquitous concern and differing rates of population are involved in the various sections of Italy, per capita treatment of the data is indicated. At this juncture, then, an attempt is made to estimate the changes that have taken place recently in the quantity of goods and services available on the average to every man, woman, and child in each area. In Table 8, regional growth is shown in per capita terms.

With the population variable included, the relative standings of income in each region are also revealed. Thus in 1951, each person in Italy had an income, on the average, of 160,000 lire.[16] This ranged from a high of almost 250,000 in the Northwest to lows of about 100,000 in the South and Sicily. A broadly similar pattern prevailed in 1960.

16. At the exchange rate prevailing at that time, this would correspond to 260 U.S. dollars, 95 U.K. pounds, 95,000 Fr. francs (old), or 1,100 Ger. marks.

Gains during the decade in percentage terms again varied widely, as
they did in the case of the gross figures in Table 7. The East Central
region once more far outdistanced the other regions. The Northeast,
Tuscany, and Sicily approximated the national average of 82 per cent.
The other three regions, the Northwest, the South, and Sardinia, however, were below the rest of the country. Of these Sardinia was substantially lower than the other two.

Table 8. *Changes in the per capita income of the regions of Italy between 1951
and 1960*

Region	Per capita income in current lire (000)		Percentage change 1951–1960
	1951	*1960*	
Northwest	246	427	74
Northeast	199	365	83
Tuscany	158	298	88
East Central	149	306	105
South	103	177	72
Sicily	100	180	80
Sardinia	130	207	59
Italy	160	292	82

Source: Tagliacarne, "Calcolo del reddito . . . gli anni 1960 e 1951," pp. 520–25; and
for the population base a straight line interpolation to July 1 of both years from census
figures of resident populations on April 21, 1936, November 4, 1951, and October 15,
1961. *Annuario statistico italiano: 1952*, pp. 23–24; and *1961*, pp. 16–17.

These findings give little support to the thesis that the more developed areas tend to grow at a slower rate than those less developed.[17]
Both in 1951 and in 1960 the Northwest and the Northeast were at
the top of the per capita income standings, but one ranked fifth and
the other ranked third in percentage change in income between the
two years. Sicily, the South, and Sardinia rested at the bottom in terms
of income in both years, while they were fourth, sixth, and seventh in
amounts of income change. The areas with the greatest advances in
per capita income were East Central and Tuscany, where income
levels were at or above the average in both years. This evidence suggests
the generalization that the stage of development may be less important
in producing growth than the conjunction of other variables in time
and place.

Tagliacarne made one foray into pre-World War II data and utilized

17. See some evidence of this in Hoover. *ob cit.*, pp. 477–79.

regional income figures for the year 1938. Comparison of these with later information gives both a longer view of economic growth and a notion of the effects of the war on Italian regional development. Before examining the figures themselves some further adjustments are necessary because of the great inflation occurring between 1938 and 1951. For this reason the data unadjusted for this variable reflect more the change in the value of money than they do the growth in income. Therefore, the ensuing data will be adjusted to constant lire of 1960 purchasing power.

Table 9. *Real per capita income in the regions of Italy, 1938 and 1951–1960 (1960 lire, 000)*

Region	1938	1951	1952	1953	1954	1955	1956	1957	1958	1959	1960
Northwest	267	288	290	297	303	324	333	350	369	386	427
Northeast	213	233	232	244	251	271	279	293	311	337	365
Tuscany	164	185	187	204	211	225	228	240	262	280	298
East Central	181	175	200	200	216	235	239	250	269	289	306
South	91	121	119	134	137	141	148	158	162	169	177
Sicily	89	117	112	143	143	145	153	167	170	176	180
Sardinia	108	152	158	173	178	175	185	189	193	198	207
Italy	168	188	189	203	209	223	230	243	256	272	292

Source: Tagliacarne, "Calcolo del reddito . . . gli anni 1960 e 1961," pp. 520–25; and Tagliacarne, "Calcolo del reddito del settore privato e della publica amministrazione nelle provincie e regioni d'Italia nel 1953," *Moneta e Credito*, VII (1954), pp. 187–89. The population base is a straight line interpolation to July 1 of each year from census figures of resident populations on April 21, 1936, November 4, 1951, and October 15, 1961 (*Annuario statistico italiano: 1952*, pp. 23–24; and *1961*, pp. 16–17). Price adjustments from national income series adapted to various bases in *Annuario statistico italiano: 1958*, p. 353; *1960*, p. 355; and *1962*, p. 353.

For the country as a whole only a very modest advance was registered in real terms over the period of war and reconstruction (Table 9). On the average each person was slightly better off in 1951 than he had been in 1938. But here again, experience varied widely. In Sardinia, the South, and Sicily substantial gains were achieved, while in the Northwest, the Northeast, and Tuscany improvements only about one third as large were reported, and in the East Central region a loss was recorded. Clearly, during the war years real per capita incomes increased more in the Southern and Insular regions than they did in the Northern and Central areas.

During the 1950's the entire nation advanced substantially. On the whole, progress differed little from region to region. The East Central section expanded most and Sardinia least, but between them the range was narrow. During the postwar period, efforts to accelerate the development of less prosperous sections of the country have produced no relative advances in these sections in comparison with the more fortunate ones. Only in the area surrounding Rome, where urbanization and governmental growth have occurred, has the region advanced notably above the others in real per capita terms.

In sum, the changes between 1938 and 1960 show greater progress for the South, Sicily, and Sardinia, the less developed sections of the country. This would support the idea that growth in less advanced regions takes place at a more rapid rate than it does in the more advanced. It is evident here, however, that the differential advantage of the less developed areas, in contrast with the remainder of the nation, lay in their experience during war and reconstruction. Thus it would seem from these figures that it was not the enlightened economic policies but the effects of war which led to a relative improvement in the South, Sicily, and Sardinia.

But these developments are better seen in graphic form. In keeping with the precision of the data, the trend lines in Chart 2 have been fitted by inspection. Joined to the lines based on the more secure information of the 1950's, broken lines representing average growth from 1938 to 1951 serve to contrast the experience between the war and recovery years with that in the 1950's. Virtually no expansion was experienced in the Northwest, the Northeast, and the East Central regions in the period described by the left-hand portion of the chart. Tuscany realized just a little gain, while Sardinia, Sicily, and the South recorded substantial progress. This means that during the war years the three less developed regions advanced, not only actually, but also relatively in comparison with the rest of the nation. In this way the per capita incomes of the regions spanned a narrower range in 1951 than they had in 1938. Looking ahead to 1960 the range is relatively unchanged, but viewed in lire terms, it spreads even further than it did in 1938.[18] In short, the period of war and recovery produced greater equality; the period of the Italian miracle did not.

18. From Table 9 actual ranges in lire of 1960 purchasing power are as follows:

	1938	*1951*	*1960*
Highest regional average	267	288	427
Lowest regional average	89	117	177
Range	178	171	250

In spite of the variety of economic growth prevailing in the parts of Italy in both the earlier and later periods, the semi-log grid of Chart 2 shows a consistent and almost North-South ranking of the regions according to per capita incomes. Of course, the patterns of Tuscany and the East Central regions are practically indistinguishable, as are those of Sicily and the South. But still there is no clear-cut example of one section overtaking and passing another. The basic elements providing the growth of each one in these two pairs of regions is quite different. The East Central-Tuscany pair is separated by the phenomenal expansion of the capital in Rome, and the Sicily-South division is accentuated by factors relating to the semi-autonomous status of Sicily. Probably

Chart 2. *Growth in real per capita income in the regions of Italy (1960 lire)*

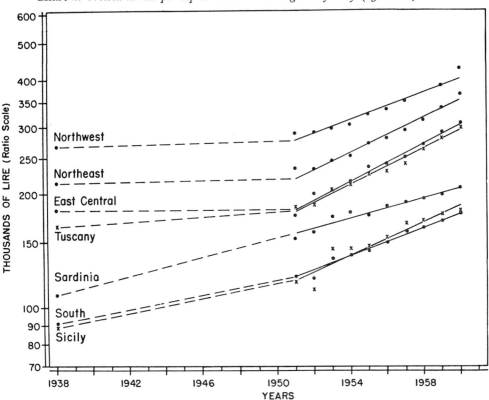

Source: Table 9. Plotted points are indicated for most regions by the symbol • ; to avoid confusion an x has been used for Tuscany and Sicily.

the regional ranking shown in Chart 2 has continued for a quarter of a century or longer.

Gaps between one region and another, even an adjacent one, are large. Thus one might think of the Northeast as lagging behind the Northwest by almost three years. In other words, if the rate of growth in per capita income continues in the Northeast for the next three years it will achieve the average experienced currently by the Northwest. Likewise the East Central region is, in turn, perhaps three years below the Northeast. Tuscany, however, is only a scant year behind East Central, but a full seven or eight years ahead of Sardinia. This, again, is the really significant gap between the developing North and the lagging South. But even below this, Sardinia's slowing advance has only brought Sicily up to within four years and the South to within five years of her level of income. As a result, even though real per capita incomes have grown in every region in almost every year, there is a continuing separation among the regions. Thus, in spite of actual improvements, relative improvements have been lacking recently.

Table 10. *Annual rates of growth in real per capita income of the regions of Italy, 1938–1951 and 1951–1960*

Region	*1938–1951*	*1951–1960*
Northwest	0.3	4.2
Northeast	0.2	5.4
Tuscany	0.7	5.6
East Central	0.0	5.9
South	2.1	4.4
Sicily	2.2	5.2
Sardinia	2.9	3.1
Italy	0.7	4.9

Source: Chart 2 and Table 9.

For a summary view of Italian regional development, numerical rates of economic growth may be compared. The straight trend lines in Chart 2 suggest exponential growths similar to the way a capital sum accrues under compound interest.[19] Because of the different overall experience of the war period in comparison with the fifties, separate rates have been computed for each. Table 10 shows these growth rates for all of the regions derived from the lines plotted on Chart 2. Rates for

19. Commensurate with the precision of the original data, the growth rates were computed from the linear logarithmic trend lines fitted by inspection in Chart 2.

Italy as a whole have been added for comparison purposes.[20] They reveal once again the gap between Northern and Southern experience. In the first period, growth was virtually nonexistent in the Northwest, the Northeast, and East Central; Tuscany did little better. In contrast the South, Sicily, and Sardinia achieved substantial gains. Clearly the period of war and recovery must be examined with care to ascertain the reasons for this divergent experience.

During the 1950's Italy as a whole grew more rapidly than the other countries of Western Europe except West Germany. Internally, high rates prevailed in all regions except Sardinia. The Rome-dominated East Central region, followed by Tuscany and the Northeast, led the other parts of the country. Closely succeeding these and still above the national average was Sicily whose relative gains advanced her in income terms above the South. Below the national average are three areas: the South, the Northwest, and Sardinia. Among these, Sardinia records the lowest rate of growth, little better, in fact, than her experience over the earlier wartime period. As a result of changes in the fifties, all regions have progressed, and progressed substantially; but the disparity in average incomes between the sections has persisted instead of declined as it had during the war period.

The questions then become: What factors in the war situation brought about the convergence of incomes? How can they be adapted to peacetime use? What factors in the postwar period produced continued divergence of average incomes? How can they be avoided in the future without jeopardizing national growth? A first step in achieving answers to these questions is an analysis of the role of population in regional development. Chapter 4 shows how this rubric gives with one hand an increased demand, a larger market, and a bigger labor force while it takes away with the other consumption and production items to feed and to equip more people.

20. Some confirmation of these results is possible by applying the same techniques to data derived by Cusimano, *op. cit.*, pp. 91–95. His estimates are generally similar to those of Tagliacarne.

II. *Components of production, development, and growth*

4. *The scope of the market*

> *The great commerce of every civilized society is that carried on between the inhabitants of the town and those of the country.*
>
> — Adam Smith

Viewing Italy as a homogeneous economic whole is like visualizing it as one great unbroken plain; no hills or valleys, mountains or gorges relieve the single expanse. When the country is divided into regions, the flat plain becomes a series of plateaus rising to the height of the average per capita income of the people living there. But this is still a coarse simile. The plateaus are not level; they are etched with the dualism of city and country life. Scattered over and rising from the plateau, then, are mounds, hills, and even mountains reflecting the higher incomes of urban centers. Thus, a first qualification of even regional homogeneity is recognition of income diversities arising with urbanization.

Cities of Italy are so venerable that they seem always to have been there. Like the pyramids of Egypt they have stood in the same place for thousands of years. It is true that some of them, such as Tuscolo, Ostia Antica, Praeneste, and Selinunte, have been abandoned because of shifting military strengths, declining ocean levels, flailing temporal rage, and changing commercial needs. But the great bulk of Italian cities of today, such as Bergamo, Brescia, and Milan, to note only a few in Lombardy, were well established centuries before their occupation by Rome (*ca.* 200 B.C.). Furthermore, they have continued to develop over the intervening millenniums for much the same economic and social reasons that exist today.

Centers of commerce, public administration, and manufacture, they furnish a market place where products and labor from the environs can be sold and taxed. Not only this, walled cities and hill-top towns provide security and a sense of pride, perhaps at times even some local chauvinism. This is understandable, for higher incomes and often more rapid rates of growth are found in key cities. For this reason, per capita incomes are substantially larger in each of the principal provinces than in their respective regions (Table 11). Thus per capita incomes, in the sample provinces chosen in Chapter 2, tend to be about equal to or lower than those of the regions as a whole.

Table 11. *Per capita income for the regions, principal provinces, and sample provinces of Italy in 1960*

			Lire of 1960 purchasing power (000)		
Region	*Principal province*	*Sample province*	*Region*	*Principal province*	*Sample province*
Northwest	Turin	Cuneo	427	503	295
Northeast	Milan	Brescia	365	600	276
Tuscany	Florence	Pisa	298	360	286
East Central	Rome	Ascoli Piceno	306	424	194
South	Naples	Salerno	177	242	178
Sicily	Palermo	Agrigento	180	201	137
Sardinia	Cagliari	Sassari	207	226	200
Italy			292		

Source: Tagliacarne, "Calcolo del reddito ... gli anni 1960 e 1961," pp. 502–25; and *Annuario statistico italiano: 1958*, p. 353; *1961*, pp. 16–17; and *1962*, p. 353.

Milan and Rome, in 1960, averaged more than twice as high per capita incomes as did the sample provinces of Brescia and Ascoli Piceno. And in Turin, Florence, Naples, and Palermo they were a quarter to a half again as great as in Cuneo, Pisa, Salerno, and Agrigento. But even more than this is suggested by the summary in Table 11. The influence of these capital cities is so great that each gives a pronounced upward lift to the income level of its surrounding region. Accordingly, living standards in the smaller cities, towns, and rural areas outside of the major metropolitan centers tend to be lower than the level for the region as a whole. They approximate more nearly, perhaps, the standards shown for the sample provinces. Thus, because of its economic and demographic importance, a major city exerts a telling influence on its entire region. This is to say that once the fabric of a plateau of average regional income is removed, the peak of its economic capital is revealed, surrounded by the hills of lesser cities and the valleys and plains of rural areas.

Differential rates of growth

At least since 1938 the ranking of the four Northern centers of Milan,

Turin, Rome, and Florence has remained unchanged. Below these leaders the per capita incomes of Southern cities and sample provinces have shifted within relatively narrow limits. So it is necessary to employ letters as well as dot and circle symbols to indicate the plotted values and to distinguish the occasionally crossing trend lines in Chart 3. Thus revealed, Cuneo, Pisa, and Brescia form a second but Northern echelon to the four leaders. While the other provinces trail in mixed ranks, Salerno and Agrigento, the sample provinces in the South and Sicily, rather consistently bring up the rear.

In terms of growth the pattern is more diversified. The high rates

Chart 3. *Growth in real per capita income in certain Italian provinces (1960 lire)*

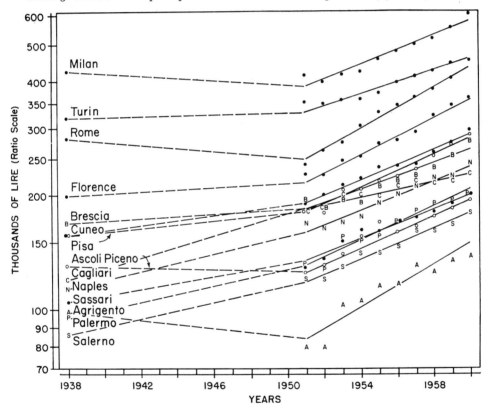

Source: Table 9 sources. For most provinces the plotted points are indicated by the symbol •. For the other provinces the following letters are used: Agrigento—A, Brescia—B, Cagliari—C, Naples—N, Ascoli Piceno and Pisa—O, Palermo—P, and Salerno—S.

of the East Central region, followed by Tuscany and the Northeast, are approached by Sicily, the South, and the Northwest (Table 12). Sardinia is conspicuously last. Provincial rankings are a different matter. As might be anticipated, the provincial capitals are bellwethers of their regions, and a comparison of rankings using Kendall's coefficient shows a significant correlation between the two listings—one, in fact, that would only occur by chance once in one hundred examples.[1] This underlines the importance of the regional metropolis in setting the tone of economic accomplishment for the entire area. Each such center acts as a harbinger of its surrounding countryside.

Table 12. *Rate of growth per year in real per capita income for regions, principal provinces, and sample provinces of Italy, 1951–1960*

			Percentage rate of growth		
Region	Principal province	Sample province	Region	Principal province	Sample province
Northwest	Turin	Cuneo	4.2	4.1	4.8
Northeast	Milan	Brescia	5.4	4.5	4.0
Tuscany	Florence	Pisa	5.6	5.7	5.1
East Central	Rome	Ascoli Piceno	5.9	6.4	4.9
South	Naples	Salerno	4.4	4.6	4.7
Sicily	Palermo	Agrigento	5.2	5.3	6.5
Sardinia	Cagliari	Sassari	3.1	2.4	4.5
Italy			4.9		

Source: Table 9 and Charts 2 and 3, and sources noted therein.

Sample provinces do not occupy this strategic role. Statistically their ranking offers no significant relationship to the ordering of regions[2] or even to the sequence of principal provinces.[3] This suggests that the sample provinces are properly only part of a considerable cross section of regional economic activity. The range of average values in the Northwest seems typical of the usual situation found here in which the rate of income growth of the region lies between the rates of the principal and sample provinces. This reason, plus the presence of a cross section of noteworthy industrial and commercial complexes, and the fact that regional income is high, makes the Northwest an appropriate

1. Kendall's score (S) is $+17$, his coefficient (τ), $+0.810$, and the probability that a value as high as τ could occur by chance (P) is 0.011. See M. G. Kendall, *Rank Correlation* (2nd ed.; London: Griffin, 1955), pp. 3–11, 49–55, and 171.
2. $S = -5$, $\tau = -0.238$, and $P = 0.562$.
3. $S = +9$, $\tau = +0.429$, and $P = 0.238$.

subject area in which to examine the influence of the scope of the market on the economy of a region.

The case of the Northwest

Forces of the past have produced in the Northwest a comparatively unique and relatively homogeneous part of Italy. By proximity, treaties, and even occupation, French influence has lent a common external tone to the region. The watershed of the Alps was not the historical boundary of the Northwest, for the Duchy of Savoy straddled the mountains to hold both Chambery of modern France and Turin of modern Italy under single rule. In subsequent years French power extended down the eastern mountain slopes to form a ring almost at the plain. Furthermore, the Kingdom of Sardinia and the French Empire at times embraced the whole of the Piedmont and Liguria, too. Although these two regions arose from common origins there is a dichotomy between the inland sections and the coastal area. The Maritime Alps on the west and the Apuan Alps or, more properly, the northern end of the Apennines on the east form an effective barrier between the Piedmont of Savoy and the Republic of Genoa. However, railroads, and more recently, power lines, pipe lines, and toll highways have enlarged commerce and communication between the two parts of the Northwest; and as trade has expanded, the area long subject to much the same general pressure of language and custom has increasingly become a single entity. Finally, within this Northwest as a whole, expanded communication facilities have permitted local specializations to develop.

Per capita incomes for the provinces of the region are relatively high and not widely diversified. So in Chart 4 there are a number of crossing situations which dictate the use once again of symbols and letters to distinguish the plotted points one from another. The lowest averages in the Northwest in 1960, as rated by Cuneo and Asti, are larger than the averages shown by all of the other sample provinces in Table 11. Higher even than the values for the principal provinces of Naples, Palermo, and Cagliari, and higher, too, than those for the entire regions of the South, Sicily, and Sardinia, these provinces with the lowest incomes in the Northwest about equal the average for the nation as a whole. This eminent position of the area is consistent with the region's place in the van of the nation's economic accomplishment.

Graphic emphasis of these characteristics is found in Chart 4. Drawn with a scale similar to those of Charts 2 and 3, it gives visual evidence of the high level and narrow path of these average incomes. The close interrelationships among the estimates and the crossings of the trend lines imply a relatively similar but vibrant area. However, the gap between Alessandria below and Novara, Savona, and the other higher income provinces suggests that upper and lower levels persist even in this relatively affluent area.

Growth is another matter. Both among the provinces of the Northwest and among the regions of Italy the range in rates of growth is

Chart 4. *Growth in real per capita income in Northwest provinces (1960 lire)*

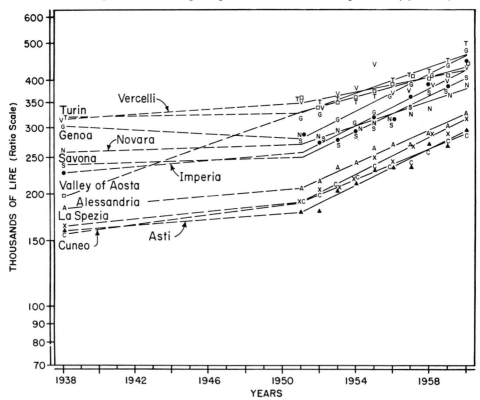

Source: Table 9 sources. Plotted points are indicated by the following symbols: Turin—T, Vercelli—V, Genoa—G, Novara—N, Savona—S, Imperia—•, Valley of Aosta—□, Alessandria—A, La Spezia—X, Asti—▲, and Cuneo—C.

great. Between Vercelli and the quadrumvirate at the top, the spread is almost three times (Table 13). Here is a significantly greater spread than those occurring among the sample provinces and the regions of Italy (Table 12), but less than the one found among the principal provinces. This evidence supports the propriety of the choice of the Northwest as a single, generally homogeneous region where a variety of forces may be examined in detail. Parts of the Northwest exhibit higher rates of income growth than the regional center, Turin. Clearly, the great port of Genoa and its neighboring coastal cities of La Spezia, Imperia, and Savona share high rates. In addition the relative hinterland of Asti, Alessandria, and Cuneo lying between Liguria and Turin, records higher rates than Turin itself. Although the "where" of higher rates of growth is easily answered, the more intriguing "why" needs yet to be attempted. In this region where incomes are comparably high and relatively uniform, what population characteristics are shared by regions with high rates of income growth?

Table 13. *Percentage rates of growth in real per capita income in provinces of the Northwest, 1951–1960*

Province	Percentage rate of growth
Genoa	5.84
La Spezia	5.83
Asti	5.77
Imperia	5.76
Savona	5.55
Alessandria	5.21
Cuneo	4.83
Turin	4.08
Novara	3.80
Valley of Aosta	3.04
Vercelli	2.23

Source: Chart 4.

Some clue to the answer to this question may be sought in the relationship between income and growth. Although the results of a previous comparison at the regional level were negative, here in a more uniform situation a significant correlation may be present. Certainly there is a definite clustering of provinces at the higher end of the scale, ranking from the top in Table 13. Among those showing high rates of income growth there is a mixture of high, medium, and low income levels

(Chart 4). This would tend to support the earlier absence of correlation. Further, a more systematic comparison using Kendall's method shows no significant association between the ranking of provinces according to rate of growth and a ranking according to average income.[4]

In relative terms, as noted previously, growth from a low income base is much easier to attain than the same growth from a higher base. Although the percentage rate of increase in each case may be the same, the actual amounts involved are vastly different.[5] Thus the lowly farmer's income in Asti may be increased by half as the result of equipping him with a modern plough, or even, of collecting all of his small parcels of land into one unbroken field. But the highly paid auto worker in Turin must be given much sophisticated and expensive automated machinery, or have the assembly line completely redesigned to achieve better material and work flows, to increase his productivity by even one quarter. This numerical aberration is probably responsible for part, but not all, of the range of growth values. Certainly if it were, Genoa would hardly be at the top. In this situation it is apparent that among the provinces of the Northwest growth and income are seemingly unrelated, and the sources of different rates of growth must be sought elsewhere.

The place of urbanization

A second fundamental factor is population. If income levels have little influence on rates of growth, the relevance of population density and growth to economic growth must then be determined. This is such a broad area of investigation that information relative to only part of it will be sought in the context of the present chapter; its relevance to such facets as the depth of capital and the supply of labor will be considered in more pertinent settings. A study of the influence of population ideally should be pursued at the communal level where more homogeneous situations can be identified. Income data, however, are not available in this detail and provincial figures must suffice. Although this size limitation is a disadvantage, even provinces display a wide range of average density of population. In the Northwest the range of densities is more than tenfold. Thus fundamental relationships are still discernible.

Four rank correlations relating population and income were examined. In two of these involving the rankings of provinces of the Northwest, no statistically significant correlations were evident. They were the re-

4. $S = -5$, $\tau = -0.091$, the normal deviate $(T) = 0.467$, and $P = 0.641$.
5. Hoover, *op. cit.*, pp. 480–81.

lations between the two static series, population density and per capita income, and between the two dynamic series, changes in population densities and changes in per capita income. In the first there appeared some slight inclination for income to vary with density. It was to such a small extent, however, that a series of chance arrangements of these values would produce this degree of relationship in about one third of the tries.

This suggests, as a first approximation, that forces may be at work in congested urban centers which tend to produce incomes no higher than elsewhere. Such influences as impediments to the smooth flow of men and materials in the port cities of Genoa and La Spezia are cases in point. With the two highest population densities of the region, they rank second and ninth in terms of income and so display a diversity of income rather than a concurrence as they would do if there were a correlation between population density and per capita income.

Part of this lack of significant relationship also may lie in the fact that population density reflects more the congestion than the size of urban centers. Both Genoa and La Spezia have high densities of population, but Genoa has four times the population size of La Spezia. Pursuing this line of reasoning further is not rewarding, however, for the size of population in a province depends in part on the area of land included within the boundaries of the province. This problem would not arise if one were dealing with a series of von Thünen's isolated states all equally sized and equally spaced, or with Lösch's original market honeycomb.[6] But here in the Northwest of Italy some provinces cover a wide expanse of fertile land, others are crowded into rocky confines, and all vary one from the other. As a result, the simple measure of population size apparently provides no clue to the working of economic growth.[7]

6. J. H. von Thünen, *Der Isolierte Staat in Bezielung auf Landwirthschaft und National-ökonomie* (Berlin: Wiegandt, Hempel & Parey, 1875); and August Lösch, *The Economics of Location*, trans. by William H. Woglom with the assistance of Wolfgang F. Stolper (2nd ed.; New Haven: Yale University Press, 1954), pp. 109–23.

7. Actual values for these four comparisons are as follows:

	S	τ	T	P
Total population (1961) to density of population (1961)	+6	+0.109	0.389	0.697
Total population (1961) to per capita income (1960)	+6	+0.109	0.389	0.697
Total population (1961) to change in density of population (1951–1961)	+3	+0.055	0.156	0.876
Total population (1961) to change in real per capita income (1951–1960)	+13	+0.236	0.935	0.350

Source: Population figures from *Annuario statistico italiano, 1961*, pp. 16–17; density of population from Table 14; per capita income from Table 15; change in density from Table 15; change in income from Table 14.

Absence of correlation was found in a second pairing when a ranking of provinces by growth in population density was compared with a ranking by growth in per capita income. Thus, growth in income seems to be unaffected by changes in population density. This suggests that other forces tend to have more influence on these separate and unique provinces than do those associated with changing population densities.[8]

Table 14. *Comparison of population density with growth in per capita income for the provinces of the Northwest, 1951–1961 and 1951–1960*

Province	Average density 1951–1961 in persons per square mile	Rate of growth per year in real per capita income, 1951–1960 (per cent)
Genoa	1379	5.84
La Spezia	690	5.83
Turin	616	4.08
Savona	418	5.55
Imperia	411	5.76
Asti	375	5.77
Alessandria	347	5.21
Vercelli	336	2.23
Novara	316	3.80
Cuneo	209	4.83
Valley of Aosta	77	3.04

Source: Chart 4; and *Annuario statistico italiano: 1951*, pp. 3, 5, and 16; and *1961*, pp. 2 and 16.

In contrast to the lack of correlation found in pairing the rankings of the two static series with each other and the two dynamic ones together, the cross-comparisons of static with dynamic series showed significant relationships. In the first of these, average population densities for the provinces of the Northwest are ranked against growths in per capita income in Table 14. Casual examination shows that the falling values in the first column of figures are matched in a general way by the declining numbers in the second. The statistical test of rank correlation is more explicit, and significantly so, for this amount of relationship would occur by chance in only two of one hundred tries. Possibly, higher densities of population provide larger markets and more versatile labor forces. Both of these conditions, by fostering economies of scale, lead to economic growth. Underlying this line of investigation has been the thought that population density might be a convenient guide to the degree of urbanization of an area. Reflecting

8. Correlation values for the first two pairings: $S = +13$, $\tau = +0.236$, $T = 0.935$, $P = 0.350$; and $S = -15$, $\tau = -0.273$, $T = 1.090$, $P = 0.276$.

a city's capacity to provide the manpower needed for production at an efficient scale, it might imply also the crowding of population necessary to muster demand in sufficient depth for specialization. The density measure, however, is not precise enough for this task. In reality the high provincial incomes do not appear to be associated with large or dense populations; they seem rather to be related to the "key" or principal cities of the region, Turin and Genoa.

Table 15. *Ranking of provinces of Northwest according to per capita incomes in 1960 and percentage change in densities of population per year, 1951–1961*

Province	Per capita income in 1960 (current lire, 000)	Change in density of population per year 1951–1961 (per cent)
Turin	503	+2.39
Genoa	479	+0.88
Imperia	450	+1.86
Valley of Aosta	442	+0.57
Vercelli	435	+0.44
Savona	405	+0.92
Novara	390	+0.80
Alessandria	328	−0.05
La Spezia	315	+0.22
Cuneo	295	−0.85
Asti	291	−0.51

Source: Tagliacarne, "Calcolo del reddito . . . gli anni 1960 e 1961," pp. 502–25; and *Annuario statistico italiano: 1951*, pp. 3, 5, and 16; and *1961*, pp. 2 and 16.

In the second correlation, changing densities of population and static levels of per capita income are involved. But instead of densities influencing income the causation seems to be the opposite. Income apparently influences densities. The functioning of the labor market may be responsible for a relationship existing between the two. Per capita income may be treated as the independent variable and change in population density as the dependent variable as they are in Table 15. The provinces are ranked according to per capita incomes in 1960. Corresponding changes in population densities between the census in 1951 and the one in 1961 are shown as a percentage change per year. Between these two listings there is a strong probability of correlation, for this amount of correspondence would occur by chance only three times in one thousand examples.[9] Thus the market mechanism ap-

9. Correlation values for the second two pairings: $S = +31$, $\tau = +0.564$, $T = 2.336$, $P = 0.018$; and $S = +39$, $\tau = +0.709$, $T = 2.958$, $P = 0.003$.

parently functions in the situation to attract workers from provinces with lower incomes to those with higher.[10]

Does a general picture emerge from these findings? Yes, but of two sorts. A restatement is in order which takes into consideration all of these relationships. In the one, local conditions are a proximate cause; in the other, the argument is more general. Population density is positively associated with income growth but not with level of income. High densities are not necessarily confined to metropolitan centers. La Spezia, ranking second in density of population, is a city of only two hundred thirty thousand, and Savona, ranking fourth, is just slightly larger. Their high population densities result primarily from location, since they are squeezed between the Northern Apennines and the Ligurian Sea. Income is average or below. Growth occurs by a spreading of economic activity outward from the burgeoning port of Genoa, but still within the brief confines of mountain and water.

A more general relationship seems to prevail in the second pair of rankings. There does seem to be some logic to the association between income levels and population growth. Certainly it would be understandable for workers from less developed areas to be attracted by the higher incomes of the urban centers. Such considerations as more diversified job opportunities, wider cultural advantages, and greater anonymity may help the high income center increase its population more rapidly than less urbanized areas.

Apparently this high rate of population growth, though it rests on high income levels, does not lead to high rates of income growth. This relationship, too, seems to correspond to other available information. With an influx of new people, the supply of labor tends to be increased and its useful efficiency tends to be reduced. A constant flow of new workers may make it unnecessary to increase wages to satisfy the demand for workers. And if productivity is going to be maintained, each new worker as he enters the local labor force must be furnished tools and other equipment at the level prevailing previously. Simply maintaining the existing level of capital plant taxes the local economy. Thus it is reasonable that rapidly growing centers do not exhibit corre-

---

10. Other reasons for migrations of this sort are summarized by Bert F. Hoselitz, "Generative and Parasitic Cities," *Economic Development and Cultural Change*, III (1955), p. 287; and compare Bernard Okum and Richard W. Richardson's thesis that no general rule can be stated on regional income inequality and the effect of migration in their "Regional Income Inequality and Internal Population Migration," *Economic Development and Cultural Change*, IX (1961), pp. 128–43.

sponding growths in per capita income. In short, the traditional urbanization movement seems to prevail here as elsewhere. But what influence has this had on the location of industry?

Varying industrial structures

Given a center of population, specialization becomes feasible. Evolution of the industries adapted to a particular urban center shapes its economic development. Beyond the blatant aspects of extractive industry and marine commerce that are delineated by geographic location, the physical characteristics of manufacturing and processing activities, as well as their products and by-products, determine much of a city's appearance. Beyond all of these distinctive features, however, are still the more specifically economic attributes that are present in demands for varied categories of labor, entrepreneurship, and materials; these demands are expressed in local wage, profit, and price levels. Thus the industrial structure, or industry mix,[11] tends to determine the profile of a metropolis in dimensions both corporeal and economic.

Even within the Northwest the range of industrial specialization is substantial. Although manufacturing is relatively most important in all but one of the provinces, the amount of emphasis on it among the other industrial activities varies from section to section and province to province. The Northwest in general and the Piedmont in particular devote attention more to manufacturing than does the country as a whole. In contrast, Liguria concentrates more heavily on commerce, especially retail trade. Because of this situation, the other details of the region already introduced, and the relative homogeneity of the area, the Northwest may continue as the subject with the emphasis now on the shaping of urban centers by industrial development.

Behind inquiries relating to the industrial profile of a city lies the economic rationale that a city, like a nation or any area, must export in order to import. Two questions are relevant here: What specialty does the area export? And, what influence does this specialty have

11. Industry mix, or the particular combination of individual industries represented in one place, is deemed by some observers to be the most important determinant of region income. Frank A. Hanna, for example, finds that about four fifths of interstate differences in average earnings are provided by the occupational composition of the labor force. Discussion of papers on regional economics, *American Economic Review*, XLV (1955), Papers and Proceedings, p. 155.

on supporting subsidiary and complementary industries, as well as those in the tertiary level? A detailed answer to the first question is possible at the national level, for careful frontier controls are maintained. At the regional, provincial, and urban levels, however, only an approximation is feasible.

One attempt to overcome the inadequacy of the data for small areas has been the recent effort to exploit the economic base concept.[12] Ratios are computed on the number of workers producing goods or services for export from the area, or "basic industry," in comparison with the number of workers producing for consumption within the area, or "service industry." One difficulty of this method lies in the impracticability of determining from existing statistics the activities properly classified in one or the other of the rubrics.

Table 16 is a case in point. The two headings employed to compute the ratios were the number of workers in manufacturing compared with the number in commerce and other activities. Falling under the manufacturing classification are extractive activities and manufacturing activities, two groups which might be included in the "basic industry" category with some justification because much of their output of granite, rice, automobiles, books, and vermouth is shipped beyond provincial boundaries. The industry classification also contains enterprises engaged in the construction of buildings, highways, and tunnels, and the installation of machinery and equipment, plus organizations producing and distributing power, gas, and water—activities primarily concerned with the local or service category. On the other side, the commerce heading embraces wholesale trade and hotels, both of which provide some of their services for export beyond provincial lines.

In spite of these and other difficulties inherent in the use of the notion of the economic base,[13] a comparison of industrial structures does illuminate the breadth of economic activity in the region. In Table 16 provinces are ranked from the top in order of importance of industry

12. Homer Hoyt, "Homer Hoyt on Development of Economic Base Concept," *Land Economics*, XXX (1954), pp. 182–86; Richard B. Andrews, a series of twelve articles on the urban economic base in *Land Economics*, XXIX (May, 1953), through XXXII (February, 1956); and Edward L. Ullman and Michael F. Dacey, "The Minimum Requirements Approach to the Urban Economic Base," *Papers and Proceedings of the Regional Science Association*, VI (1960), pp. 175–94, are examples of the copious development of this topic.

13. Hans Blumenfeld, "The Economic Base of the Metropolis," *Journal of the American Institute of Planners*, XX (1955), pp. 114–32, presents a cogent analysis of shortcomings inherent in the employment of the economic base idea.

in comparison with commerce and other activities for the year 1951. Vercelli shows the greatest concentration with three and one-half times as many workers engaged in industry as in other occupations. This contrasts with Imperia which has little more than half as many in industry as in other fields. Broadly, the upper part of the list contains provinces of the Piedmont and the Valley of Aosta, while the lower part includes mostly those of Liguria. Emphasis is thus given to the dichotomy within the Northwest between the northern part and the southern, between the industrial concentration and the commercial.

Table 16. *Ranking of provinces by ratio of the number of workers in industry to the number in commerce and other activities compared with average per capita income for provinces of the Northwest in 1951*

Province	Ratio of workers in industry to those in commerce and other activities	Per capita income in 1951 (1960 lire, 000)
Vercelli	3.51	350
Valley of Aosta	3.21	355
Novara	2.92	287
Turin	2.75	351
Alessandria	1.61	207
Savona	1.45	278
La Spezia	1.35	191
Asti	1.25	179
Genoa	1.15	316
Cuneo	1.07	190
Imperia	0.56	286

Source: Annuario statistico italiano: 1952, pp. 203–4; 1953, pp. 195, 196, 242, and 255; 1954, p. 247; 1955, pp. 216–17; 1957, pp. 199, 242, 264, 266, 267, 269, and 307; 1958, p. 353; 1959, p. 160; 1960, p. 355; and 1961, pp. 16–17, 160, and 164–69; and Tagliacarne, "Calcolo del reddito . . . gli anni 1960 e 1961," pp. 508–10.

Provinces arranged in the order found in Table 16 show a slight positive rank correlation with a listing of them according to levels of per capita income.[14] Thus higher incomes seem to be associated with greater concentrations on industry at a probability level of seven in one hundred. Historical developments support this finding. Rapid postwar reconstruction had taken place; by 1951 a less spectacular but more consistent growth began to accrue, price levels which had been fluctuating began to stabilize, and industrial production which had been increasing rapidly settled down to a slower rate of expansion. In short, the census of 1951 marks the first year after the war that can be classi-

14. $S = +24$, $r = +0.436$, $T = 1.791$, and $P = 0.073$.

fied in economic terms as relatively normal. Thus the time immediately prior to 1951 was a period of rapid change in which the market mechanism played an important role in channeling needed labor to areas of new development. In this situation the evidence of a greater degree of industrialization being associated with higher incomes may reflect the upgrading of local workers previously underemployed or unemployed, plus the movement of more skilled, higher paid workers to provinces where their talents were required by the newly created or expanded establishments.

This relationship did not persist. Trial rank correlations between industrial structures in 1961 and levels of income in 1960 show no apparent relationship.[15] Perhaps changes during the fifties were less thoroughgoing than they were in the late forties. Certainly the absence of correlation reflects not only a narrowing of differences in industrial structure and a relative decline in the range of per capita incomes, but also the influences of many economic, political, and social forces dictating a march of people toward the city and a shift of manufacturing to the country.

One leveling force is the increased use of bargaining by national councils to set uniform wage levels for broad areas. Under this system the market functions less efficiently. Although higher wages than those set by these agreements are paid by some employers, distinct sectional patterns persist especially among newer and weaker firms.[16] The unwillingness of individuals to shift from one employer to another without sufficient financial reward, the reluctance of many classes of workers and their families to migrate to new surroundings, and the presence of continuing areas of large-scale unemployment and underemployment may tend to bring about a relative migration of industry. New firms, new plants for old ones, new expansions of existing branches, and new sources of parts and subassemblies are located in areas with a favorable

15. Even a revised listing of provinces, in which construction and production of power, gas, and water were moved to the "all other" category leaving the heading "industry" to include only extractive and manufacturing, proved no better than correlations employing the broader industry definition of Table 16. Values by Kendall's method are the same for comparisons of per capita income figures for 1960 with both the structure ratios by the definition employed for those in Table 16 and those suggested above: $S = +1$, $\tau = +0.018$, $T = 0.000$, and $P = 1.000$.

16. George H. Hildebrand, "The Italian Parliamentary Survey of Unemployment," *American Economic Review*, XLV (1955), p. 895, and Giuseppe Ammassari, *I salari di fatto in Italia* (Milan: A. Giuffrè, 1963), found among the largest industrial firms that there was a substantial disparity between contractual wage scales and actual wages paid. Payments above contractual wages were found to have a pronounced geographic distribution, with the spread between the urban centers and rural communities and between North and South being especially large.

labor supply. Frequently this means placement in less densely populated areas, often within easy transportation reach of existing industrial concentrations.[17] But this is only an hypothesis explaining the lack of correlation between industrial structure and income change: can it be supported by the facts of industrial change?

For Italy as a whole the relative importance of the three broad categories of industrial activity remained virtually unchanged between 1951 and 1961. In the Northwest, however, there was a notable decline in manufacturing, offset by an increase in other activities including transportation, communication, finance, and public services. To bring this about, the two major parts of the Northwest developed in contrasting ways. The Piedmont traded a relative decline in commerce for an increase in other activities, and Liguria exchanged a decline in manufacturing for an increase in commerce. Carrying the breakdown one step further, among the six provinces of the Piedmont the importance of manufacturing declined relatively in the more industrialized provinces and increased both relatively and actually in the less industrialized.

Table 17. *Comparison of changes in density of population and changes in structure of industry for the provinces of the Northwest, 1951–1961*

Province	Change in density of population per year 1951–1961 (per cent)	Change in structure of industry 1951–1961 (per cent)
Turin	+2.39	− 2.2
Imperia	+1.86	0.0
Savona	+0.92	−13.1
Genoa	+0.88	−12.2
Novara	+0.80	− 8.2
Valley of Aosta	+0.57	−38.6
Vercelli	+0.44	−12.0
La Spezia	+0.22	− 4.4
Alessandria	−0.05	+ 5.6
Asti	−0.51	+24.0
Cuneo	−0.85	+25.2

Source: Table 15; and *Annuario statistico italiano: 1952*, pp. 203–204; *1953*, pp. 195, 196, 242, and 255; *1954*, p. 247; *1955*, pp. 216–17; *1957*, pp. 199, 242, 264, 266, 267, 269, and 307; *1959*, p. 160; and *1961*, pp. 160 and 164–69.

To support this hypothesis, movement of new industry toward rural areas should be evidenced by an inverse correlation between shifts in population density and variations in industrial structure. Table 17 lists the provinces of the Northwest in declining order of change in population density, with Turin at the top showing a gain of more than

17. Lösch, *op. cit.*, pp. 182–92, especially 183 (note).

2 per cent per year and Cuneo at the bottom suffering a loss of almost
1 per cent each year. A reverse of this population movement took place
in the shift in industrial structure, as Turin's concentration on manufacturing showed a slight decline and Cuneo's registered a large advance.[18] Between the two rankings of the provinces as a whole, there
is an inverse relationship that would have happened by chance in six
of one hundred instances.[19] Thus there is modest evidence of a relative movement of manufacturing from areas of growing to areas of
falling population density.

The simple facts that population densities are so high in Italy, that
there are so many well established towns, and that well conducted local
transportation effectively extends the scope of the market make population density of itself less important to the economy than it is in newer
countries. The findings concerning industry structures, per capita incomes, and population densities are of a piece, however. The shift in
people toward the large "key" centers in search of higher incomes
through greater job opportunities is now matched by a movement of
industry in the reverse direction in an attempt to utilize other sources
of unemployed labor. Attempting to remove local wage incentives from
the functioning of this market by national agreements tends to make
the mechanism less efficient, as solutions are attained primarily by a
shifting of quantities rather than by movements of both prices and
quantities as might otherwise prevail.

Discussion thus far has centered largely on questions relating to the
size and distribution of population. And rightly so, for the number of
persons in the economy and their location play crucial parts in determining average income and market scope. Still another aspect of
population, touched only obliquely thus far, awaits more careful consideration. This is the role of population in providing the labor factor
of production.

---

18. Not all of the changes in structure were the result of increases in the manufacturing
classification. Between the censuses of 1951 and 1961, the movement of population from
provinces with lower densities of population to those with higher was accompanied by a
shift in the number of workers in commercial enterprises serving them. This produced
relatively less expansion in commercial activities among provinces with declining densities
and an actual reduction in their number in the case of Cuneo where persons engaged in
commercial enterprises in 1951 numbered 29,598 while in 1961 they totaled only 29,117
(estimated from *Annuario statistico italiano: 1955*, pp. 216–17; and *1961*, pp. 164–65).

19. $S = -23$, $\tau = -0.418$, $T = 1.868$, and $P = 0.061$.

5. *The labor force: structure and capacity*

> *The three problems of the age—the degradation of man by poverty, the ruin of women by starvation, and the dwarfing of childhood by physical and spiritual night.*
> — Victor Hugo

By what measures does one view a labor force? If by size, then one would say that the Italian labor force was large in embracing some twenty-two million persons at the last census in 1961. But this is a rather meaningless figure when set off by itself without reference to the economy as a whole. Perhaps the single, most enlightening value is the one relating the size of the labor force to the size of the total population. It is by this percentage that the number of workers for money wages is set off against the number depending on them. By this measure, the proportion was found to be 43 per cent in Table 6. A second commonly used measure concentrates on the adult population and specifies the ratio of the active population to the total population aged fifteen to sixty-four. However, since there is a regional pattern of employment of persons younger than this in Italy and since the definition of adult varies from place to place, the labor force to total population figures have been used here generally. But the other measure fills in a distinct part of the picture and shows that roughly two of three adults are gainfully employed in Italy, a participation midway in the range when Italy is ranked with other Western European nations, the United States, and Canada, where the numbers run from 61 to 76 per cent.[1]

---

1. In 1960 the ranking for percentage of population aged 15 to 64 in the labor force was as follows:

Denmark	76	*Italy*	*67*
France	74	Sweden	66
United Kingdom	72	Canada	63
West Germany	72	Norway	63
Switzerland	70	Netherlands	62
United States	68	Belgium	61

Source: Derived from Angus Maddison, *Economic Growth in the West* (New York: Twentieth Century Fund, 1964), p. 31.

Both the strength of social custom and the level of economic opportunity lie behind this figure for Italy. Women in general do not work in paid occupations; thus only 27 per cent of the labor force is female in comparison with a high of 37 per cent for West Germany and a low of 25 per cent for Canada.[2] Furthermore, many persons of both sexes in the labor force are engaged in occupations below the level of their training.[3]

Used in this way, these are static measures of the existing status of the active population at this moment in time. Variations in these figures, on the other hand, tend to indicate changes in the labor force as a factor of production in the economic potential of the whole economy. Hence an increase in the proportion of the population gainfully employed, *ceteris paribus,* leads to both a larger national product and a greater per capita income since more work is put forth in the overall and the income of the individual employed need be shared with fewer persons in the particular. A gain has not been shown in Italy; although the population of the country has almost doubled in the last century, the labor force has only expanded by one third.[4] Thus, the proportion of the population gainfully employed has declined substantially.

Italy is, as has often been said, a study in contrasts. This chapter, too, is a study in contrasts, but not of all of her varied regions, for this would be too cumbersome for effective analysis at an exploratory level. Rather, it is a study in contrasts between the labor force of the Northeast and the labor force of Sicily. It is a juxtaposition of unlike situations, but not polar extremes. If the latter had been wanted, the provinces of Milan and Cosenza would have been chosen as those ranging most widely in

2. Italy ranks relatively low in this regard. Percentages of labor force consisting of women in 1960, in the nations reporting comparable information among those just referred to, are as follows:

West Germany	37	Switzerland	30
Sweden	35	*Italy*	27
United Kingdom	34	Norway	27
United States	32	Canada	25
Belgium	30		

Source: Ibid., p. 33.

3. See, for example, comments by George H. Hildebrand, "The Italian Parliamentary Survey of Unemployment," *American Economic Review,* XLV (1955), p. 889; and Commissione Parlamentare di Inchiesta sulla Disoccupazione, *La disoccupazione in Italia* (Rome: Camera dei Deputati, 1953), I, Pt. 2, pp. 18–19, 20–21, and 302.

4. Marcello Boldrim, "Un Secolo di sviluppo della popolazione italiana," in *L'Economia italiana dal 1861 al 1961* (Milan: A. Giuffrè, 1961), pp. 35–61; and Francesco Coppola D'Anna, "Le forze di lavoro e il loro impiego in Italia," in Commissione Parlamentare di Inchiesta sulla Disoccupazione, *op. cit.,* IV, pp. 5–73.

income levels. Instead, two larger regions are employed—the North-east and Sicily; they cover the general range of income effectively, yet do not reflect such unique situations that generality is lost.

In the Northeast are two centers of commercial eminence: Venice, long the imposing link between West and East; and Milan, her histor-ical rival and recent hub of Italian business activity. Beyond this the re-gion includes an arc of industrial cities—Padova, Vicenza, Verona, Brescia, and Bergamo—which straddle the ancient trade route between Venice and Constance. Within it also lies Ravenna, one-time capital of the Eastern Empire; and there are a host of lesser agricultural, trade, and industrial provinces in which much early trade union activity took place, especially in Lombardy, Romagna, and Emilia.

In contrast, Sicily is an island, but one closely linked to the Mainland. Presently one of the five sections of the country possessing a considera-ble degree of political and economic automony,[5] it has functioned under such diverse controls as Saracen, Spaniard, and Savoyard. Although in the past two thousand years its culture has not achieved the architec-tural splendor of the period of Grecian domination, Sicily has been a center of social developments, marked by Garibaldi's victory at Palermo and including notable organizations of peasants and laborers.

The structure of the labor force

Many influences from the past and the present determine the form and character of the labor force in Italy. Powerful frictions impede the resolution of stresses to form a single labor market from the diverse re-gions of the country. Thus Northern Italy in general and the Northeast in particular is made up of a structure of small towns and hamlets on which has been superimposed a series of regional urban centers. Oppos-ing this in the Southern and Insular sections typified by Sicily is a net-work of agricultural towns averaging two to three times the area of those in the Northeast on which is layered, also, a system of larger cities.[6] In either instance the nature of town life, developed centuries ago by eco-nomic, military, and political expediency, shapes much of the present character of regional differences.

Original and continued heavy dependence on agriculture has been an

5. Others are: Friuli and Venezia Giulia, Upper Adige, Valley of Aosta, and Sardinia.
6. See Folke Dovring, *Land and Labor in Europe, 1900–1950* (The Hague: Martinus Nijhoff, 1956), especially the map facing p. 15.

omnipresent influence. First in shaping the dissimilarities between the areas was the contrasting place of farming in their economies. In very early times subsistence farming was, of course, the basic source of income in all regions; but soon the specialization of *cittadini* became increasingly evident. In the Northeast this found expression in industrial and trade developments when such items as metal objects from Tuscany and bronze implements from Bohemia passed in commerce. Effort and capital flowed into these ventures instead of into greater extensions of agriculture, for although the Po Valley is extraordinarily fertile, sizable investments were needed to clear its forests and control its flooding before it could be used. Thus in seeking an export of value, location and resources dictated trade and industry along with agricultural produce.

In Sicily the easily pulverizable soil and the wishes of Grecian colonists determined the emphasis on grain as an exportable crop. Wine and cheese were shipped abroad as well, but these, too, required slight local processing so that the economy was little moved to develop supporting industry and services of any consequence. These varied economic environments in the two regions generated contrasting labor structures. The Northeast called forth a smaller agricultural population than Sicily.[7] Consequently in the Northeast more workers and more capital entered commerce and industry, and in time the activities supporting them flourished, too. In Sicily, on the other hand, emphasis on cash crops which required little processing produced a less diversified economy. On top of this, especially large *latifundia* in Sicily produced a wealthy, often absentee, landowning class which found little incentive to invest in anything but land, buildings, and non-risk avenues generally.[8]

Even in the philosophy of the regions this diversity finds expression. In contrast with the Puritan norm of the essential goodness of toil, there is an aspect of *la bella figura,* or image of appearance and conduct, which looks with distaste on mundane effort. This latter view finds origin in the ancient world where free citizens looked down on manual toil as the work of slaves. Probably four fifths of the working men, both skilled and unskilled, in Roman times were slaves and ex-slaves.[9]

7. Gunnar Meckivity, "Medieval Agrarian Society in Its Prime," in Vol. I of *The Cambridge Economic History of Europe,* eds. J. H. Clapham and Eileen Power (6 vols.; Cambridge: Cambridge University Press, 1944), p. 336.
8. J. S. Macdonald, "Agricultural Organization, Migration and Labour Militancy in Rural Italy," *The Economic History Review,* 2nd series, XVI (1963), p. 70.
9. Tenny Frank, *An Economic History of Rome* (2nd ed.; London: Jonathan Cape, 1927), pp. 324–27.

Thus, in spite of some protestations to the contrary by Vergil,[10] the premium on military exploits, the gifts of grain, and the availability of talented slaves brought into disuse and even disrepute essential requisites of economic growth, craftsmanship, and entrepreneurship.

In addition to the prevailing aversion to toil, there is also a local antipathy to trade and industry prevalent in the South.[11] Dating at least from Roman times when neglect of these occupations contributed to imperial decline, this antipathy contrasts with the espousal of industry and trade which has existed in Tuscany and the North of Venice and Genoa at least since the inauguration of metal workings by the Etruscans in the ancient world.[12] Modern vestiges of these aversions and predilections also are reflected in the structure of the modern working population.

Table 18. *Percentage distribution of the employed labor force in the Northeast and Sicily according to type of occupation, September 8, 1952*

	Northeast	Sicily
Agriculture, including hunting and fishing	36	47
Industry, including extractive, manufacturing, construction, and electric, water, and gas utilities	38	25
Commerce, including credit and insurance	12	10
Transportation and communication	3	5
Other, including varied services and government	11	13
Total	100	100

Source: SVIMEZ, *op. cit.*, pp. 601–2.

Table 18 illustrates the fundamental ambivalence of the two labor forces. Many influences of geographic location, political antecedents, available resources, and social mores lie behind these figures. The structure of the gainfully employed shows a heavy preponderance of farmers, hunters, and fishermen in Sicily where almost one half of the working population pursued these endeavors in 1952. This is in spite of the fact that the Northeast encompasses much of the Po Valley, the most fertile part of Italy. Where today an acre of valley land along the Po yields twenty-six bushels of wheat, an acre in Sicily yields only thirteen.[13] Yet, one half of the gainfully employed in the Northeast were engaged in industry and commerce, while only 35 per cent of those in Sicily were

10. Vergil, *Georgics*, I, 121–46.
11. Other material supporting this thesis is noted by Clough, *op. cit.*, pp. 166–67; and Margaret Carlyle, *Modern Italy* (London: Hutchinson University Library, 1957), p. 99.
12. D. Randall-MacIver, *The Etruscans*, pp. 1–33; and Block, *op. cit.*, pp. 83–115.
13. Meckivity, *op. cit.*, p. 324.

employed in these areas. And this is not a recent development, for as early as the thirteenth century the nonagricultural part of the population was proportionately larger in the Northeast than in Sicily.[14]

More can be learned by examining the sex-occupational composition of the population in Table 19. Here, using more recent decennial census data of 1961, the dissection of the labor force is taken one step further. In comparison with Sicily, a larger proportion of males in the total population are in the labor force of the Northeast. This situation results from a variety of influences which include the following: Population is growing faster in Sicily than in the Northeast; thus there are more males who are too young to have entered employment as yet.[15] There are fewer job opportunities for older workers in Sicily than in the Northeast; thus retirement takes place at an earlier age. Competition for existing work is stronger in Sicily than in the Northeast; thus more young persons and marginal workers do not even attempt to find gainful employment and devote themselves instead to subsistence activities.

Table 19. *Percentage distributions of men and women in the Northeast and Sicily according to occupational classifications in 1961*

	Men		Women	
	Northeast	*Sicily*	*Northeast*	*Sicily*
Labor force	75	70	25	12
Agriculture	17	27	3	5
Industry	37	23	11	1
Commerce	11	8	8	3
Other	10	12	3	3
Not in labor force	25	30	75	88
Total population	100	100	100	100

Source: *10° Censimento generale della popolazione, 15 ottobre 1961*, III, Appendice, pp. 28–31.

Reflected in the data these same influences affect the proportion of women in the labor force. There is the additional factor that women are dissuaded in large numbers from seeking employment because of the established Sicilian mores against their working.[16] The logic may be that it is just not proper for one of them to take a scarce job away from a man who is the breadwinner or prospective breadwinner of a

14. *Ibid.*, p. 326.
15. By the simple measure of the excess of births over deaths, population in Sicily is growing currently twice as fast as it is in the Northeast. *Annuario statistico italiano: 1962*, pp. 15–16 and 28–30.
16. Franco Archibugi, "Recent Trends in Women's Work in Italy," *International Labour Review*, LXXXI (1960), p. 293.

family. These and other impressions are gained from an examination of the age structure of the gainfully employed in Table 20.

Table 20. *Percentage of population in age and sex groups gainfully employed, 1951*

	Men		Women	
Age	*Northeast*	*Sicily*	*Northeast*	*Sicily*
10–13	10	21	7	3
14–20	68	72	45	7
21–44	95	92	36	10
45–64	90	87	20	12
65 and over	45	39	5	5

Source: IX *Censimento generale della popolazione, 4 novembre 1951*, IV, pp. 572–78, and 588–89; and VII, pp. 126–32, 142, and 205.

Restraints on achieving full employment are reinforced by the very presence of unemployment. Clearly, smaller proportions of males aged twenty-one and over are employed in Sicily than in the Northeast. This results from the absence of job opportunities and constitutes disguised unemployment, for the incidence appears not in the unemployment totals themselves, but in the lower labor force participation rates. Less participation in the labor force means first less of the labor factor of production and second—under the ideal conditions of full employment and of *ceteris paribus* needed for preliminary analysis—a smaller total product, at least that part of the total product reflected in the market place. This measured output is augmented in part by more home care, gardening, and self-sufficiency in general. This is an explanation of the statistics rather than a support of the system, since in this situation many specialized tasks are performed by each individual, a notably in-efficient practice. In this way the lower labor force participation in Sicily reduces its possible income in both figure and fact as non-priced goods are produced by less efficient means.

As contrasted with the smaller proportion of older men, there is a larger proportion of younger males in the labor force in Sicily. The working of several influences brings more youths aged ten through twenty into the active population. Absence of a high level of employ-ment has its bearing as more boys are forced to obtain work to help support their families. Then too, there is not the same antipathy toward employing boys as there is toward hiring girls and women; after all, if the boys are not now the heads of families they soon may be. Also, it is cheaper to employ boys, especially those under fourteen years of age.

Wages and supplementary wage payments for dependents are lower for younger workers. Beyond this the younger boys are in a *sub rosa* situation to begin with, for the law requires them to attend school until they are fourteen years of age.[17] Although this age group has been found to function efficiently in industry, these Sicilians usually work in agriculture.[18] It seems to be easier to disregard a law of this type on a small, rural farm than in a large, urban factory. By a longer view, the greatest influence of this sizable employment of youths is the loss to them, and thus to the labor force, of years of training. With advancing automation, unemployment is found increasingly among the untrained and unskilled workers, while job openings persist for the trained and skilled.

Lack of employment opportunities for women is the *bête noire* of the South. An essential feature of the economic difficulties of Sicily and the South and Insular regions in general stems from the fact that they have been unable to utilize the available individuals in the labor force. This is especially true of the female part of the population. As seen from Table 20, only 3 per cent, 7 per cent, 10 per cent, 12 per cent, and 5 per cent of the possible number of workers at the various age levels are actually employed. Of course many of these persons have responsibilities in the home which preclude their working for someone else. But this accounts for only a small part of the large differences between the percentages for the Northeast and Sicily. Only among the oldest age group, those sixty-five and over, does the percentage given for Sicily equal the one for the Northeast. In this case need again plays a role in the distribution, as well over half of these elderly working women are widows.[19]

Changes over time in the structure of the labor force have worked against rather than for the relative economic improvement of Sicily in comparison with the Northeast. The figures just discussed in Table 20, though published in 1957 and 1958, actually date from 1951. Reference to Chart 2 shows that this year marked the end of a period of substantial relative improvement for Sicily in comparison with the Northeast. Gains since then, though appreciable, have not been large enough

17. The original law of 1923 was incorporated into the Constitution of 1948. See Margaret Carlyle, *op. cit.*, pp. 82–99, for a discussion of how it applies to Italian education in general.

18. In the age group ten to fourteen, 72 per cent were in the classification farming, hunting, and fishing in 1951. Istituto Centrale di Statistica, *IX Censimento generale della popolazione, 4 Novembre 1951* (Rome: Fausto Failli, 1957), IV, p. 605.

19. Istituto Centrale di Statistica, *Dati generali riassuntivi*, Vol. VII of *IX Censimento generale della popolazione, 4 Novembre 1951* (Rome: Azienda Beneventana, 1958), p. 142.

to bring the sections closer together in economic terms. Thus in the recent past, since the complete details of a census were published, structural changes may not have improved the disposition of the labor factor of production.

In the broader scope, the relative position of Sicily seems to have deteriorated since the *Risorgimento*. Although the proportion of the population gainfully employed in both areas has declined, the Northeast did start from a significantly higher base, especially among women. Furthermore, changes in the occupational structure tended also to work against Sicily. In ninety years the Northeast, particularly in the case of men, developed a labor force structure much in keeping with industrialized populations elsewhere. Involvement in industry increased markedly, in agriculture it declined significantly, and in commerce there was some expansion. The "other" category, including varied services and government, declined. The growth in the industrial sector is especially noteworthy, for it started from 16 per cent of the total male population, or 22 per cent of the male labor force in 1871.[20]

In Sicily among the males, there have been only modest changes except for the movement from agriculture. Although the industrial base approximated that of the Northeast in 1871, there has been little expansion since then. But a closer view is possible in Table 21. Here the ninety years since Unification are divided into two parts: 1871 to 1951, the pre-miracle period of modern Italian development, and 1951 to 1961, the miracle period itself. In both the earlier and the later one, changes are shown in the percentages of men and women in the total population engaged in various activities. Perhaps the most important phenomenon illustrated is the flow of workers out of gainful employment. Typical of all except women in Sicily during the recent past, this movement reflects a variety of influences among which longer schooling and earlier retirement are noteworthy. It bespeaks a higher living standard and a greater reliance on social security schemes, and is reflected in the lower unemployment totals of other statistical series. This trend continued in both areas during the recent period of the miracle, when the outflow of men from agriculture was mostly to non-remunerative pursuits, especially in Sicily where the three percentage points gain in industry was to a low 23 per cent (Table 19).

Elsewhere Table 21 records that a large number of women in both sections left the labor force in the earlier period. This, too, suggests

20. Sources noted in Table 21.

Table 21. *Percentage points of change in distributions of men and women in the Northeast and Sicily according to occupational classifications, 1871–1951 and 1951–1961*

	1871–1951		1951–1961	
	Northeast	Sicily	Northeast	Sicily
	Men		Men	
Labor force	−9	−2	−8	−11
Agriculture	−24	−4	−14	−15
Industry	+12	+2	+3	+3
Commerce	+6	+6	+3	0
Other	−3	−6	0	+1
Not in labor force	+9	+2	+8	+11
	Women		Women	
Labor force	−22	−21	−4	+3
Agriculture	−23	−3	−5	+2
Industry	−1	−15	−1	+1
Commerce	+6	+2	+3	0
Other	−4	−5	−1	0
Not in labor force	+22	+21	+4	−3

Source: *Popolazione classificata per professioni, culti e infermità principali, Censimento 31 dicembre 1871*, III, pp. lxviii–lxix; *IX Censimento generale della popolazione*, IV, pp. 597–605 and 784–97; and *10° Censimento generale della popolazione, 15 ottobre 1961*, III, Appendice, pp. 28–31.

higher income levels. However, the jobs they left differed; in the North-east they gave up agriculture, in Sicily it was industry. The economic implications of this diversity are profound, for in one many of the women accompanied their families from farm to factory, while in the other the cottage industry was curtailed and nothing took its place.[21] Behind this substantial decline in the employment of women in Sicily lies a long downward trend which started between the census in 1881 and the one in 1901. At the first census 18 per cent of the total female population was employed in industry; by the second it had fallen to 5 per cent.[22] This period of twenty years marks a substantial turn in the economy of Sicily. The Crispi regime was involved in a tariff war with France, there was a serious decline in the textile industry, Italy experienced her greatest depression, and a series of successful strikes occurred in Palermo. In addition, the role of women in industry was changed. The social inadvisability of wage employment was stressed. Pope Leo XIII said in his *Rerum novarum* (1891), for example: ". . . a woman

21. Note a development of this theme in Archibugi, *op. cit.*, pp. 293–97.
22. SVIMEZ, *op. cit.*, p. 44.

is by nature fitted for home work and it is that which is best adapted at once to preserve her modesty, and to promote the good bringing up of children and the well-being of the family." [23] And, legislative actions increased the cost of employing women. The Act of 1902 outlawed night work for young women, required that women receive one day of rest each week, and directed firms to allow women room and time to nurse their children.[24] In the end Sicilian women were no longer widely employed in industry.

From this brief review of the existing vocational structure of the population and its changes in ninety years, it is evident that the working force in the Northeast is relatively more numerous than it is in Sicily. The main cause of this is the lower rate of participation of women in Sicily. In addition to this, there have been occupational shifts toward higher paying industrial work in the Northeast and toward lower paying agricultural effort in Sicily. Thus, structural changes, by providing a larger and better paid labor force in the Northeast, have tended to enlarge the regional economic differences with Sicily.

Table 22. *Percentage of total population gainfully employed in the regions of Italy, 1952 and 1964, and changes therein*

Region	1952	1964	Change 1952–1964
Northwest	45	44	−1
Northeast	45	44	−1
Tuscany	44	41	−3
East Central	41	40	−1
South	37	36	−1
Sicily	32	32	0
Sardinia	32	32	0
Italy	41	40	−1

Source: *Annuario statistico italiano: 1953*, p. 330; and *1965*, p. 353. Because of differences in the inclusiveness of national and regional data, the national averages of regional values shown here are not exactly the same as the overall national averages shown in Table 6 which include individuals temporarily working abroad.

Similar structural and size contrasts are evident elsewhere. The ratio of the labor force to the total population is a convenient measure of this pattern. In Table 22 it shows the greater participation of the population in gainful employment among the Northern regions where the numbers follow the general North-South listing of the regions in the

23. Quoted by Archibugi, *op. cit.*, p. 301.
24. *Ibid.*, p. 307 (note).

table. They reveal an unbroken sequence from high to low with a 45 per cent rate in the Northwest and the Northeast balanced by a 32 per cent rate on Sicily and Sardinia, with intermediate levels in the intervening regions. Small changes occurred between 1952 and 1964 with declines evident in all but the islands. As reflected by these data, the structure of the labor force and its relative size continue to exhibit profound regional variations, variations which account for a portion of the previously noted income differences.

The amount of unemployment

Economic status of the labor force presents much the same problem as the question of economic growth in Italy as a whole: both involve regional differences with broad ramifications. The problem of economic growth is narrowed to workable proportions here by use of selective sampling. Discretion must also be used in selecting the particular facets of the general question of labor to be passed over quickly and those on which to look with care. An example of the first of these is the topic of unemployment. In principle it is of major concern to the whole discussion, but in practice even ascertaining the actual numbers involved may be quite another matter. Since the facts are so difficult, if not impossible, to learn, a prolonged discussion at this stage has limited usefulness.

Choice of the base from which to measure the numbers of persons who are not working is crucial. As has been noted in the data relating to the structure of the labor force, the persons employed and actively seeking employment in Sicily represent a much smaller proportion of the total population than they do in the Northeast.

Of basic moment to the economy is the size of its labor force. More specifically, it is the proportion of the total population gainfully employed. This term embraces those who are actually working as well as those who are looking for work.[25] This is not an ambiguous concept, and it is an easy definition for the census taker to utilize. For the student interested in the economic realities of the situation it is less than

---

25. In terms of definition the "labor force," or the "gainfully employed," or the "*popolazione attiva*" includes persons who were employed at the time of the census in a profession or occupation, or who had lost a position and were in search of a new one, or who were temporarily prevented from working by military service, condition of health, or confinement in prison up to five years. Excluded from the gainfully employed category are youths in search of their first jobs, students, pensioners, prostitutes, those permanently disabled, persons confined to prison for five years or longer, persons of independent means, and women who keep house. See *IX Censimento generale della popolazione*, VII, p. 8.

satisfactory, however, for it fails to record the numbers of persons who have given up trying to find work because no opportunities seem to exist, or the women who have never sought employment because it is no longer socially proper to do so.

What is important in the broad view needed at this juncture is some knowledge of the latent size of the labor force. If there are not sufficient jobs to employ this number, this is a problem to be examined subsequently. At the moment the essential answers to be sought are: What is the potential size of the labor force? How much of this potential is being utilized?

Table 23. *Comparison by sex of population, labor force, and persons on unemployment rolls for the Northeast and Sicily, 1963*

	Northeast	Sicily
Men		
Population	8,299,000	2,305,000
Labor force	5,183,000	1,292,000
Persons on unemployment rolls	177,774	101,918
Percentage of population in labor force	62.5	56.1
Percentage of population on unemployment rolls	2.1	4.4
Percentage of labor force on unemployment rolls	3.4	7.9
Women		
Population	8,690,000	2,378,000
Labor force	2,300,000	286,000
Persons on unemployment rolls	131,007	26,791
Percentage of population in labor force	26.5	12.0
Percentage of population on unemployment rolls	1.5	1.1
Percentage of labor force on unemployment rolls	5.7	9.4

Source: Annuario di statistiche provinciali: 1963, pp. 284–87.

Very roughly, the number of workers in Sicily could be increased by one third. Table 23 contains the raw materials of this approximation. The population and labor force figures are based on estimates as of October 20, 1963; those for the unemployment rolls are averages for the calendar year 1963 of the number of persons listed in local employment offices who are classified as unemployed workers, individuals over twenty-one years of age in search of their first occupation, and housewives in search of their first job.[26] Assuming that these figures repre-

26. Maddison, *op. cit.*, pp. 218–19, notes that these figures may contain some upward bias since the lists are maintained by local authorities whose grants from Rome depend partly on the size of their unemployment rolls. Even this, however, would hardly negate the validity of their use to show regional differences. The unemployment rolls themselves include two other categories of listings not incorporated in the totals used here; they are pensioners in search of work and employed individuals looking for other jobs.

sent the population, the labor force, and the unemployed by sex, Table 23 may be used to rationalize the situation a step further. First, by simple numbers the unemployment lists are much longer in the Northeast than they are in Sicily. But this is not of much interest in itself, for there are also a greater number of people and a larger labor force in the Northeast. The answer in relative terms differentiates the two regions: 2.1 per cent of the male population in the Northeast is found on these rolls, while 4.4 per cent is recorded on the Sicilian rolls. More significant still is the relationship between the labor force and the unemployment lists; the percentages this time are 3.4 and 7.9 for the Northeast and Sicily, respectively. The unemployment picture among the women in both areas is even worse; the comparable values of the labor force are 5.7 and 9.4.

Regardless of the base used, however, comparisons of unemployment lists alone may not be too meaningful. As has been noted, for a variety of reasons many persons may not be counted in the labor force: although they would like to work they may have given up looking for a job, they may never have had the training needed for employment, or they may have been dissuaded from seeking work because of the social mores against the gainful employment of women. The extent to which these people would expand the labor force if they were given the opportunity to work is not easy to judge. The very differences in the populations of the regions make for contrasting practices. If, however, these are disregarded for the moment and the populations of the Northeast and Sicily are assumed to be similar, an approximation of the potential size of the labor force is possible.

Taking the structure of the labor force in the Northeast as a norm, the labor force in Sicily may be measured against it. In the Northeast, 62.5 per cent of the male population is in the labor force, but in Sicily the figure is only 56.1 per cent. This difference of 6.4 percentage points means that almost 150,000 men in Sicily are not included in the labor force, although they would have been in the Northeast. Among the women the difference in Table 23 is 14.5 per cent; this amounts to nearly 350,000 persons. How many among these groups of men and women should be counted among the unemployed? Certainly some of them are children, some of them are mothers of young children, and some of them are too old to work; but certainly, also, some of them would enter the labor force if they thought an opportunity for work existed or if they thought it was socially proper. Thus in total, perhaps half a million persons might conceivably be added to the unemployment rolls, or more hopefully, to the labor force of a full employment economy.

Table 24. *Percentage of labor force unemployed in regions of Italy, 1952 and 1964, and changes therein*

Region	1952	1964	Change 1952–1964
Northwest	6	1	−5
Northeast	7	3	−4
Tuscany	7	2	−5
East Central	7	3	−4
South	6	3	−3
Sicily	7	3	−4
Sardinia	7	3	−4
Italy	7	3	−4

Source: Annuario statistico italiano: 1953, p. 330; and *1965,* p. 353. The 1952 sample was based on a single sample dated September 8, 1952; the 1964 results were adjusted to an annual average from monthly figures from January, April, July, and October. Some modifications were made in the coverage between the two dates.

This same reasoning could be followed for the other regions of the country. Instead, with the reservations concerning the nature of these unemployment registration figures in mind, it is appropriate to look at other data of the regional distribution of unemployment to see how they have changed recently. Table 24 summarizes the published results of national samplings of unemployment in 1952 and 1964. It shows that during the earlier year unemployment was rather evenly distributed throughout the country, holding at 6 or 7 per cent of the labor force. By 1964 this figure had declined to 3 per cent in most regions and to 1 and 2 per cent, respectively, in the Northwest and Tuscany. This imparts a taste of North-South differences, but maintains in the other five regions a notable uniformity in both prevailing rate and amount of reduction. Since the weight of this accumulation of evidence implies that there is a large unutilized sector of the population which might engage in profitable employment, some attention needs now be given to why these people are idle. First concern may be directed to the training received by this group in particular and by the population in general.

The place of education

Amintore Fanfani, as Premier in 1958, introduced a far-reaching plan to reorient and expand Italy's lagging educational system.[27] In spite of internationally acknowledged successes by some Italians in such diverse fields as physics and economics, the traditional emphasis of the system has been on the humanities through high school and on law at the university level. In spite of the provision of the Constitution requiring that children attend school for at least eight years, many youths leave school and seek employment much earlier than the law provides. Thus the supply of trained natural and social scientists, teachers, and even skilled technicians is grossly short, especially in the South and particularly among the women there.[28]

Except for the five semi-autonomous regions, the educational system is nationally centralized. Although local communities provide buildings, decisions concerning the curriculum, textbooks, examinations, and other vital aspects of the scheme are made in Rome. The minister of education at the head of the organization appoints a superintendent of schools (*provveditore agli studi*) for each province, who in turn works through a number of supervisors (*soprintendenti*), who in their turn deal with a much larger number of teaching principals (*direttori didattici*) who not only teach but also direct groups of schools. In short, the clear line of authority extends from the teacher in the classroom to the ministry in Rome.

Even in subject terms the educational structure is fully prescribed. In all except the art and music schools, which may be entered at the end of four or five years in the elementary grades, the basis of the educational pyramid is the compulsory eight years of work composed of five years in elementary school and three years in either a vocational or a liberal arts junior high school. From here the trade-oriented students go on to technical schools or professional institutes, and spend from two to five years completing the work in such areas as agriculture, industry, marine occupations, or home economics. The graduates of liberal arts junior high schools can go on to specialized high schools in classics, sciences, arts, teacher training, and technical subjects. Four or usually five years at these *licei* or *istituti* lead to the normal schools, the acade-

27. Difficulty associated with implementing educational reforms is evidenced by the fall of the government over state aid for private schools in June, 1964.
28. Margaret Carlyle, *op. cit.*, pp. 82–99.

mies of fine arts, and the universities.[29] Advancement from grade to grade and from school to school is conditioned by the passing of rigorous examinations which significantly narrow the field at each successive level. These qualifying examinations are administered from Rome.

Two sorts of statistics are illuminating at this juncture: one compares the distribution of students currently enrolled in the two regions being compared, the Northeast and Sicily, and the other examines the way education has changed since the *Risorgimento*. In general, the educational system is one of extremes. Selection of a career is made very early. Entrance into the music conservatories, for example, may be at the end of the fourth grade of elementary school, or at about ten years of age. And even the basic choice between the vocational and the liberal arts programs on which all subsequent selections hinge is made at the end of the fifth grade. This dichotomy between the two types of training—the trade school and the university preparatory—is a very real one; it involves a highly specialized vocational training in the one and a traditionally based liberal arts education with classical emphasis in the other.

At the end of three years at the junior high level (about age fourteen), a number of more specific choices must be made as to the area in which the ultimate profession will lie. Beyond this point only students electing the high school of classics (*liceo classico*) and the high school of science (*liceo scientifico*) may select from a considerable number of areas of specialization at the university. Thus early selection of an ultimate goal and early involvement in professional subjects are two characteristics of the Italian educational system.[30]

Partly as the outcome of this early specialization, partly as the development of the Gentile reform,[31] and partly as the result of the traditional veneration of a few professions, the Italian educational system lends a unique occupational profile to its labor force. In comparison with the current emphasis placed on the natural sciences and engineering elsewhere, the Italian system tends to stress law, the social sciences, and

29. A helpful schematic diagram of these arrangements is shown facing p. 98 in *Annuario statistico italiano: 1965*.

30. For a discussion of the influence of this professionalism in one area, see Eugenia C. Saville, "Current Chronicle: Italy," *Musical Quarterly*, XLVI (1960), pp. 371–80.

31. See Merritt M. Thompson, *The Educational Philosophy of Giovanni Gentile* (Los Angeles: University of Southern California Press, 1934), pp. 5–20, for a discussion of this reform during the early days of Italian Fascism and a characterization of Giovanni Gentile, the philosopher, who was Minister of Education under Mussolini.

the humanities. These are areas that Giovanni Gentile, the philosopher of fascism, sought to resuscitate in his support of absolute idealism, in place of the positivism and naturalism stressed in the later nineteenth and early twentieth centuries. And despite the degree of centralized control, regional patterns of results differ markedly.[32]

Table 25 tells much of the story. Here the specializations of the elite at the top of the educational pyramid are compared for the Northeast and Sicily. With subject areas ranked in order of numerical importance in the Northeast, the sequence of fields of concentration at the university is apparent. First, the area of the social sciences includes economics, business, and political science; a concentration of students in Milan and Venice brings about this atypical situation. Within the pure science category are mathematics, physics, and miscellaneous natural sciences; in the medical sciences are medicine, surgery, and pharmacology. The humanities represent literature and philosophy, while agriculture involves the usual panoply of the agronomist plus veterinary medicine.

Table 25. *Number and percentage distribution according to subject area of students at the university level in the Northeast and Sicily for the academic year 1960–1961*

	Number		Percentage	
Subject area	Northeast	Sicily	Northeast	Sicily
Social sciences	16,472	4,391	29	19
Engineering and architecture	8,802	969	16	4
Pure sciences	8,112	2,712	14	12
Medical sciences	7,875	2,677	14	12
Law	5,679	6,370	10	28
Education	4,514	3,008	8	13
Humanities	4,003	2,350	7	10
Agriculture	920	492	2	2
Total	56,377	22,969	100	100

Source: *Annuario statistico italiano: 1962*, p. 116.

Sicily's more traditionally Italian approach is evident. Over one quarter of all of her university students are specializing in law, almost one quarter in the natural sciences, less than one fifth in the social sciences, one tenth in the humanities, and less than one twentieth in engineering and architecture. The brightest comparison, the emphasis on teacher training, is tarnished somewhat by the knowledge that concentration here reflects not so much a demand for this subject area as the

32. *Ibid.*, pp. 1–3 and 21–35.

absence of available educational alternatives, especially for girls.[33] Finally, in both regions only one fiftieth of the students at the university are in the field of agriculture.

A similar pattern appears in a minor key at the lower reaches of the educational structure. The broadly based pyramid starts in the elementary years with virtually 100 per cent of the population in the age group six to eleven attending school. This percentage shrinks in successive steps, reaching 5 per cent at the university level.

Regional differences in behavior extend even to this contraction process. In Sicily the initial decline in the proportion of persons attending school takes place earlier than it does in the Northeast. This situation is evident from Table 20 in which a much larger proportion of boys aged ten through thirteen were gainfully employed in Sicily. At the same time, more of the students remaining in school there continue to the university level. As a result, a significantly larger proportion of the population attends the university than in the Northeast.[34] At least three influences have brought about this situation. First, at the age level of from eighteen to twenty-four or twenty-five—the time students normally attend the university—job openings in Sicily are fewer than they are in the Northeast. Since the employment advantages possessed by the younger boys aged ten through thirteen do not apply to this older group, the opportunity cost to them of attending the university is lower than it would be in the Northeast. Second, the early school dropouts may take many potential candidates for vocational training out of the educational system. Among those remaining there may be a more customary preference for university work. And third, this may be evidence of a more stratified distribution of economic opportunity. As one of the characteristics of less advanced areas, the upper class may attend the university in large numbers, for it is one aspect of *la bella figura*.

Changes in educational emphasis appear over time. In actual numbers the size of the student body at the university has increased since 1926. Relative to the expanding size of the population there has been a general advance as well. As seen in Table 26 the proportion of the population attending the university in Sicily has been larger than it has been in the Northeast. And what is perhaps more important, the attendance has

33. Carlyle, *op. cit.*, p. 97 (note).
34. Comparison of data in Table 25 with age-population figures in *IX Censimento generale della popolazione*, VII, pp. 126–30, 132, and 142, and general population data in *Annuario statistico italiano: 1962*, pp. 17–18.

increased more in Sicily than it has in the Northeast. This was not a smooth advance in either place, and especially not in Sicily. There, the proportion of students more than doubled between the academic years 1936–37 and 1950–51, whereas only a modest advance took place between 1950–51 and 1960–61. This is further evidence of the high relative advance of Sicily in the period marked by World War II in comparison with the last decade.[35]

Table 26. *Number of persons per thousand in total population in the Northeast and Sicily attending the university in specified years*

Academic year	Northeast	Sicily
1926–1927	1.0	1.2
1936–1937	1.6	1.8
1950–1951	2.6	4.7
1960–1961	3.4	5.0

Source: SVIMEZ, *op. cit.*, pp. 12, 828–29, 832–33, 836–37; and *Annuario statistico italiano: 1962*, pp. 15, 16, and 116.

Subject emphasis within the university changed, also. In actual numbers there was an increase in every major division between the mid-1920's and the early 1960's. This was by no means a continuous or uniform development, however, and fluctuations in student numbers in several disciplines appear from period to period. In Table 27 these changes are shown in percentage terms. Ranked according to their standing in the Northeast during the academic year 1926–27, the subject areas show a heavy concentration in the medical sciences. The second place standing of law and the scant attention given to education are also noteworthy, in the case of law because of its traditional status and in the case of education because of its subsequent development. Results of Gentile reforms and Fascist policies are evident in expansions of education, humanities, and social sciences as against declines in engineering, pure science, and agriculture.

Revisions occasioned by World War II expanded in the Northeast the areas of engineering and architecture and pure science at the further expense of law, agriculture, the humanities, and education. During the last decade the most dramatic shift has been the decline not only in the proportion, but also in the actual numbers of students in the medical

35. See Chart 2 and related discussion of relative income gains among the regions in the two periods.

Table 27. *Percentage distribution of students attending the university in the Northeast and Sicily according to subjects for selected years*

	Northeast				Sicily			
	1926–1927	*1936–1937*	*1950–1951*	*1960–1961*	*1926–1927*	*1936–1937*	*1950–1951*	*1960–1961*
Medical sciences	31	28	29	14	31	20	21	12
Law	16	13	11	10	25	28	25	28
Social sciences	15	22	20	29	11	18	11	19
Engineering and architecture	14	10	16	16	3	3	8	4
Pure science	10	6	10	14	20	6	13	12
Agriculture	7	4	3	2	1	1	2	2
Humanities	6	11	8	7	7	12	13	10
Education	1	6	3	8	2	12	7	13
Total	100	100	100	100	100	100	100	100

Source: SVIMEZ, *op. cit.*, pp. 12, 828, 829, 832, 833, 836, and 837; and *Annuario statistico italiano: 1962*, pp. 15, 16, and 116.

sciences. This is offset by substantial increases in the areas of the social sciences, pure science, and education.

In Sicily something of the same pattern of development is repeated. The emphasis on law is substantially greater both in the twenties and throughout the time shown in Table 27. Also, engineering and architecture begin with a much lower base than they had in the Northeast. The Gentile and Fascist influences, also, produced great changes in the university structure in Sicily, with expansions in law, social sciences, humanities, and education. By the beginning of the fifties, however, pure science ranked above the Northeast in the percentage of students included. Engineering and architecture expanded more than twofold in percentage terms and many times in actual numbers. In 1960–61 the impressive previous gains in the sciences were not maintained. In fact, registrations in the medical sciences declined in relative importance as did those in engineering and architecture. The relative standing of pure science, engineering and architecture, and agriculture—areas which might be thought to be of much help in the economic development of the region—constituted one quarter of the students in the university in 1926–27; some thirty-odd years later they involved slightly more than one sixth of them. Thus evolutions from the past have led the Northeast to achieve an educational profile apparently more in keeping with current economic and social development than the one now exhibited by Sicily.

Table 28. *Proportion of men and women age six and over in the Northeast and Sicily unable to read in 1871 and in 1961, and changes therein*

	Northeast		Sicily	
1871				
Men	52		79	
Women	65		91	
Total		58		85
1961				
Men	2		15	
Women	3		17	
Total		3		16
Change in percentage points, 1871–1961				
Men	−50		−64	
Women	−62		−74	
Total		−55		−69

Source: Ufficio Centrale di Statistica, *Popolazione classificata per età, sesso, stato civile ed istruzione elementare, Censimento 31 dicembre 1871* (Rome: Tiprografia Cenniniana, 1875), II, pp, 250–60 and 292–95; and *10° Censimento generale della popolazione, 15 ottobre 1961*, III, Appendice, pp. 24–27.

These modifications in the orientation of the university transpired at the apex of the educational pyramid. Other and broader changes took place at the lower levels of this structure as well. One concrete outcome of this is the wider dissemination of literacy in the population. The symbol of the political party and the proclivity for abbreviations are in part responses to the fact that a large segment of the population was unable to read at all or read only with difficulty. Table 28 shows something of the remarkable progress that has been made in extending this basic skill.

At the time of Unification nine out of ten women and eight out of ten men in Sicily were unable to read. Conditions were better in the Northeast where only two thirds of the women and about one half of the men were in this category. Conditions vastly improved in the next ninety years. Almost all of the people in the Northeast had learned to read and about five out of six in Sicily had developed this ability.

In many ways the educational system has improved the capacity of the labor force to do productive work. Almost all of them have been taught the basic skill of reading. Many other advances have been made toward better fitting them for gainful employment. As measured by the programs of the university in training the elite of the labor force, the actions in the Northeast seem to have been more thoughtfully directed toward fulfilling the requirements of a modern technical society than those in Sicily. Chapter 6 continues the investigation of the labor force of these two contrasting regions with regard to its organization and cost. This leaves until Chapter 7 consideration of the role of education as a signal element of investment for economic development.

6. *The labor force: organization and cost*

Financially impoverished, poorly organized, deficient in supporting strength among the category federations, and impotent in collective bargaining, the present labor movement, like its predecessor, has also invested its meager fortunes in political gambles.

— Maurice F. Neufeld

By Western standards a labor force of average size functions in Italy. It is decidedly not a homogeneous body. Between Sicily and the Northeast there is a divergence of structure in terms of sex, age, and occupation. Even in training there are influential variations. How have these differences been mirrored in the development of labor organizations? Very briefly, the developing unions are characterized by a difficulty in differentiating between political action and collective bargaining, by an uncertainty about central control and local responsibility, and by an absence of exclusive bargaining arrangements and the multiplicity of arrangements thereby entailed.

The organization of the labor force

For a number of reasons the Italian labor movement has led a frustrating existence. First there was the time before the *Risorgimento* when foreign domination and an un-unified country led to repeated suppression and to fragmentary developments. Then under the new nation there was legal opposition to organization and strikes.[1] Later under Fascism and war, unions although nominally important had little opportunity to bargain or to strike. Still later, after World War II, national organization became splintered into parts of varying hue, and union strength was used as a political as well as an economic weapon. Finally the ambient of an underemployed labor force and a tradition of wage settlements at the national level have tended to remove collective bargaining from the tool kit of unions.

1. See Shepard B. Clough, *The Economic History of Modern Italy* (New York: Columbia University Press, 1964), pp. 151–56, for a discussion of the relevant penal code section, Articles 385 and 386.

Both the Northeast and Sicily were responsible for goodly portions of early union efforts. In Emilia under the La Marmora government in 1866, twenty-six peasants were killed and fifty-five wounded in uprisings against a tax on flour.[2] In Palermo under the Kingdom of the Two Sicilies strikers for higher wages among bakers and shoemakers in 1850 were referred to as mutineers (*ammutinamenti*), and about one hundred of the more difficult workers were deported to a nearby island.[3] These actions resulted from organizations in many trades, especially textiles, and among agricultural workers.

Political and economic action in Italy are inexorably intertwined. Concurrent formation of a unified nation and a labor movement took place under conditions of wide hostility and active government suppression. Furthermore, the leaders of one were often the spokesmen of the other. Thus Giuseppe Mazzini, the patriot and the associationist, worked for both the political unity of Italy and the organization of Italian workers.[4] A rival of his, Mikhail Bakunin, led the International in Italy and sought the adoption of a truly revolutionary base.[5]

In response to Mazzini's adaptation of the teachings of Robert Owen, a co-operative movement mushroomed into some twenty thousand societies. Allied with socialist and trade union activities this branch of the labor movement was heavily concentrated in the Northeast, particularly in Ravenna, Reggio Emilia, and Bologna.[6] In Sicily the vast *latifondi* and their administrators, the *gabellotti*, gave rise to agricultural co-operatives which rented large estates and so dispensed with this class of intermediary managers.[7]

By the turn of the century the split between the idealism of Mazzini and the anarchism of Bakunin had crystallized, and the Italian labor movement was divided in two parts. At this point the chance joining together of groups hostile to political action—the syndicalists, the republicans, the anarchists, the regionalists, and the extreme left-wing

2. Humbert L. Gualtieri, *The Labor Movement in Italy* (New York: S. F. Vanni, 1946), p. 77.

3. *Ibid.*, pp. 6–7.

4. For details of his *Patto di fratellanza* see Gastone Manacorda, *Il movimento operaio italiano attraverso i suoi congressi* (Rome: Rinascita, 1953), pp. 48–75.

5. Gualtieri, *op. cit.*, pp. 54–70; and Daniel L. Horowitz, *The Italian Labor Movement* (Cambridge, Mass.: Harvard University Press, 1963), pp. 17–23.

6. E. A. Lloyd, *The Co-operative Movement in Italy* (London: Allen and Unwin, 1925), p. 34.

7. *Ibid.*, pp. 81–83.

socialists—led to a victory for them. Successful in opposition, this heterogeneous group was paralyzed in power.[8]

During this situation of inaction, a congress of labor was held in Milan during the last days of September and the first days of October, 1906, creating the Confederazione Generale del Lavoro. The effect of this organization, as modified in congresses in Mantua during 1914 and Leghorn in 1921, was to amalgamate local associations into large countrywide and district-wide groups. Thus a truly centralized organization was in effect by the advent of Fascism.[9]

With Fascism, control of labor moved firmly to the right. In 1925, after branding the strike of metal-working unions originating in Lombardy an act of war, the Grand Council saw to the passage of a measure outlawing strikes and lockouts and making the National Confederation of Fascist Trade Unions the ultimate spokesman for labor. Here, again, a strong central body was in control of organized labor; even non-members were required to pay dues. Labor courts acted as arbitration panels, and many national contracts were in effect.[10]

Since World War II the labor movement has again become divided, this time into four major groups. Partly because the beginnings of labor organization were so mingled with actions for Unification, partly because there has been a traditional emphasis on such inter-craft organizations as city labor councils (*camere del lavoro*), and partly because there was such a strong partisan emphasis under Fascism, these labor organizations are distinguished more by their political associations than by their activities in a purely labor context.

Thus the two ideological extremes are occupied by a pair of unions. The communist-dominated Confederazione Generale Italiana del Lavoro, or more usually CGIL, developed from a mixed group in 1944,[11] and finds its strength among the mechanical and engineering industries where relatively high wages are paid. The neo-Fascist Confederazione Sindacati Nazionali Lavoratori, or CISNAL, has few members and

8. Rinaldo Rigola, "The Reconstruction of the General Confederation of Labour in Italy," *International Labour Review*, III (1921), pp. 261–62.

9. *Ibid.*, pp. 262–72.

10. Clough, *op. cit.*, pp. 230–34; and G. Lowell Field, *The Syndical and Corporative Institutions of Italian Fascism* (New York: Columbia University Press, 1938).

11. The General Confederation of Industry, the General Confederation of Agriculture, the Confederation of Labor, and the Catholic Italian Confederation of Workers. See Clough, *op. cit.*, pp. 353–54, for further details.

little industrial importance. Between these two is a second pair of labor organizations. The larger, the Confederazione Italiana Sindacati Lavoratori (CISL), is allied with the Christian Democratic party and associated with the Church. It was founded in 1950 from the Federazione Italiana del Lavoro (FIL) which had seceded from the CGIL a year earlier and from a Catholic group, the Libera Confederazione Generale Italiana dei Lavoratori (LCGIL). The smaller of the middle-road unions is the Unione Italiana del Lavoro (UIL), which is allied with the Social Democrats.

Political affiliations of this order mean that much of the energy of labor organizations is devoted to non-labor matters.[12] This fact—coupled with the very number of competing unions; their practice of operating on limited budgets because of the tradition against substantial dues; and the system of double contract negotiations, once for basic issues at the national level and once for supplementary matters at the local level—leads to very complex conditions in the labor market. That half of the labor force is not unionized only adds to the number of variables, as the unorganized segment follows more or less quickly the leadership of the unions.

The incidence of strikes

One indication of union activity is found in the statistics of strikes. Although in the Italian scene they tend to be called for political reasons, work stoppages do show even here something of the power and aggressiveness of unions. Thus, like the labor movement itself, the strike in Italy is dichotomously bound to political as well as economic ends. Like the labor movement, also, the strike has gone through several characteristic phases.

Until 1889 unions were illegal and strikes were outlawed, unless workers could show a reasonable cause for striking.[13] From the turn of the century until World War I unions, and consequently strikes, developed rapidly. More members, stronger unions, and better organization produced bigger and more effective strikes. Notably, larger general strikes were employed. In 1904 the "five days of the dictatorship of the proletariat," and in 1914 *la settimana rossa* or "the red week" were

12. For an elaboration of this point of political involvement, see Maurice F. Neufeld, "The Inevitability of Political Unionism in Underdeveloped Countries: Italy, the Exemplar," *Industrial and Labor Relations Review*, XIII (1960), pp. 363–86.
13. See Articles 385 and 386 of the Penal Code, and Clough, *op. cit.*, p. 151.

outstanding examples of this union device.[14] In the first, a version of the sit-in strike was employed in an effort to secure some voice for labor in management councils; and in the second, the general strike was used to protest the assignment of military conscriptees to disciplinary battalions. Such strikes were inspired more by political than economic motives and involved regions, sections, or industrial segments rather than the nation as a whole. They did serve a very significant purpose, however, in indoctrinating Italian labor and the nation as a whole into the acceptance of the idea of the general strike. Although the number of man-hours lost because of strikes averaged about twenty-three million per year during the first decade of the century, the gains were not evenly dispersed among the labor force. In fact, urban and Northern workers gained more than the rural and Southern groups; as a result differences between city and country and North and South were augmented by the labor movement.[15]

Between the two world wars union activity was drastically curtailed. Immediately after World War I the strike rate resumed at a lower level than in the period prior to the war. Occurring chiefly among workers in textiles, railroads, and metal trades, the issues were wage increases, minimum wages, the nationalization of industry, the establishment of factory councils, and the eight-hour day. Expanding momentarily during the first few years of the Fascist regime, the general strike which originated among the metal workers in the Northeast in 1925 was the culmination of the movement. It was its consummation as well, for in 1926 the Rocco Law was passed which established new settlement procedures for labor disputes and outlawed strikes.[16] Evidence of the status of strikes during the next eighteen years appears not with other data relating to the labor force as it does presently, but as *conflitti* listed under the heading for crimes. In this instance they are "crimes against the public economy, industry, and commerce—for strikes and lockouts." The number of workers convicted was notably small.[17]

14. Clough, *op. cit.*, pp. 154–56.
15. Adapted from Lutz, *op. cit.*, pp. 208–9.
16. Clough, *op. cit.*, pp. 208 and 232–33.
17. "Delitti contro l'economia pubblica, l'industria e il commercio—per scioperi e serrate":

Year	Number	Year	Number
1933	101	1935	70
1934	71	1936	23

Annuario statistico italiano: 1938, pp. 296–97.

Following World War II strike action was again intensified.[18] Once again political stance motivated many strikes, particularly those inaugurated by the Communists who, adhering to the leadership in Moscow, opposed aid from the United States, the NATO alliance, and other efforts designed to improve Italy's stature. In this recent period the incidence of strikes in the Northeast and Sicily has developed differently. As seen in Table 29, in both 1950 and 1960 the number of hours lost in the Northeast was much greater than in Sicily. Nevertheless, the direction of change was different. The occurrence in the Northeast was both actually and relatively smaller at the end of the decade than it was at the beginning, while in Sicily it was larger at the end by either measure.

Table 29. *Hours of work lost through strikes in the Northeast and Sicily, 1950 and 1960*

	1950		1960	
	Northeast	*Sicily*	*Northeast*	*Sicily*
Number of hours lost in strikes (000)	32,210	1,583	26,156	3,745
Per cent of total hours worked lost in strikes	0.19	0.05	0.14	0.10

Source: *Annuario statistico italiano: 1953*, pp. 330 and 334; and *1961*, pp. 332 and 335.

Because the number of hours lost through strikes varies considerably from time to time, it is dangerous to place too much emphasis on figures for single years. In general these two years are fairly typical for the country as a whole where the total losses in 1950 and 1960 approximated the ten-year average of about forty million hours. The importance of the Northeast in this national total is substantial.

By removing the influence of the size of the labor force—one of the major contrasts between the two regions—from the raw figures in Table 29, a clearer view of the strike variable is obtained. Thus in the second row of figures Sicily had for 1950 in percentage terms only about one quarter as much time lost in strikes as the Northeast. By 1960, contrasts had narrowed. The hours lost in the Northeast declined while

18. Joseph A. Raffaele quotes a union official of CILS in Sicily as saying: "The workers have a serf complex. . . . We have to increase our strike activity in order to give them a sense of battle." *Labor Leadership in Italy and Denmark* (Madison: University of Wisconsin Press, 1962), p. 131.

those in Sicily doubled. These findings are consistent with the growing strength of union activity in Sicily and the South.[19]

The cost of labor

Labor costs, like other phenomena of the Italian scene, diverge in many ways. While within regions and between regions notable differences continue, attempts to narrow these variations by legislation have tended to perpetuate and enhance them rather than to erase them. Recently the situation has been aggravated to some extent by the reduction in tariff barriers under the European Economic Community. Thus in spite of, or perhaps because of, national and supernational efforts toward uniformity, Italian labor costs, too, continue sectional individuality.

Italian labor costs versus Western European labor costs. If the comparison is confined to wage earners in a sample of manufacturing industries, labor costs in Italy are generally lower than they are in the other Common Market countries. More specifically, out of seventeen industries including iron and steel, automobiles, textiles, paper, chemicals, and rubber, Italian labor costs including fringe benefits were lowest in thirteen. In three, the Netherlands was the only country showing lower costs than Italy, and only in the rubber industry were Italian costs higher than those of all the other Common Market producers: France, Belgium, West Germany, and the Netherlands.[20] Thus, for wage earners in manufacturing industries, labor costs are generally lower in Italy than they are in the other countries of the European Economic Community.

These findings are based on a study of larger establishments, those employing fifty or more persons. Broadly speaking, the size distribution

19. For a general statement in English of the problem of Italian labor organization, see Maurice F. Neufeld, *Italy: School for Awakening Countries* (Ithaca, N.Y.: Cayuga Press, 1961).

20. Cesare Vannutelli, "Labour Cost in Italy," *Banca Nazionale del Lavoro: Quarterly Review*, XV (1962), p. 371. His findings are based on a study by the Statistical Institute of the European Economic Community in *Bulletin of Social Statistics*, No. 3 (1961), for the year 1959. The industries in question are: sugar, brewery, wool spinning, cotton spinning, synthetic fibres, paper, chemicals, rubber, cement, majolica and ceramics, machine tools, electrical machinery, shipbuilding, motor vehicles, pit-coal mines, iron mines, and iron and steel. "Labor cost," as used in the text, follows Vannutelli's definition, the payments by the employer per unit of labor time for wages and fringe benefits. The sticky problem of comparing wage costs internationally is handled by a simple conversion of national rates in local currencies into Belgian francs as follows: 1 DM = 11.96 Belgian fr.; 100 old French fr. = 10.19 Belgian fr.; 100 lire = 8.05 Belgian fr.; and 1 Fl = 13.24 Belgian fr.

of these firms was similar for Italy, France, and Belgium. Those located in Luxembourg were decidedly smaller, while those in West Germany and the Netherlands were somewhat larger. At least a greater proportion of the firms in these last two countries were in the one-thousand-workers-and-over class than in the other Common Market nations.

Included in these figures are not only direct wage costs, but also such other expenses as bonuses and gratuities, remuneration for days not worked, contributions for social security, social taxes, expenditures on recruiting and training labor, payments in kind, and other social contributions.[21] The split in the total wage cost between direct wages and the panoply of bonuses, social security payments, and other expenses associated with the hiring of workers varies from country to country. Here again, Italy is unique. Her direct wages are the smallest percentage of total labor cost of any of the other nations in the group. Viewed from the other side, her added costs bulk largest among these nations. Thus, bonuses and gratuities and payments for days not worked average 9 per cent of total wage costs each (or 18 per cent), social security contributions run an additional 25 per cent, and miscellaneous items average another 5 per cent to bring the total to almost 50 per cent. In this way the Italian worker receives less visible remuneration and his employer a greater weight of quasi-fixed charges than do their counterparts in the European Community.[22]

Another division exists. This time it is between wage earners and salaried employees. So far the discussion has been confined to wage earners, or persons on a piece-work, hourly, or daily rate basis—as opposed to salaried employees, or foremen, supervisors, and executives, except those in the very top managing-director echelon. In Italy this general supervisory group makes up a smaller proportion of the total personnel than elsewhere in the Common Market. Furthermore, the remuneration of this group in Italy is higher than it is in other countries in the group.[23] Although persons looking at this phenomenon through Marxist eyes see an example of exploitation, the scarcity of skilled supervisors, the place of the line of demarcation between wage and salaried classes well up on the income scale, and the presence of an ever-waiting supply of unskilled and semiskilled labor provide valid reasons in market terms for the existence of this seemingly unfair treatment.

21. Vannutelli, *op. cit.*, p. 359.
22. *Ibid.*, pp. 364–65.
23. *Ibid.*, pp. 357–69.

Beyond this static view of the levels of wages and salaries existing momentarily, there are the changes in them taking place over time. In the recent past, Italian labor costs have been falling in actual as well as relative terms. During the period from 1950 to 1962, the trend of unit labor costs for Common Market wage earners in manufacturing production was very slightly downward. In none of these situations was the trend uniform. In the case of Italy, for example, it was generally downward from 1952 to 1962, and then it began climbing to reach the level of several years earlier.[24]

Bearing on wages as costs and, especially, on wages as income are the number of hours worked per week. The industrial labor force in Italy worked an average of 42.3 hours per week in 1959. This is a low estimate when compared with information available from other Common Market and Western nations. In fact, only the United States and Canada were lower; Norway, Sweden, Denmark, France, West Germany, the United Kingdom, and Switzerland ranked progressively higher, with the Netherlands at the top recording 48.3 hours per week.[25]

Looking back during the decade of the 1950's shows the long-term downward trend in hours worked being interrupted briefly here and there by cyclical fluctuations. There are several exceptions to this general decline in hours. The Netherlands remained high and almost constant, while the United Kingdom, France, and Italy each increased very slightly.[26] In summary, Italian industrial workers not only exhibit the lowest unit labor cost and receive the smallest proportion of this cost as take-home pay, but they also work a shorter number of hours per week than their counterparts in the rest of the European Economic Community.

Northeastern labor costs versus Sicilian labor costs. In general, wage patterns are set both geographically and occupationally in a series of national agreements. The large labor confederations noted previously bargain with three principal and several smaller employers' associations representing agriculture, industry, and commerce.[27] The contracts are usually for two years and involve wage rates made up of a staggering

24. John H. Chandler and Patrick C. Jackman, "Unit Labor Costs in Eight Countries Since 1950," *Monthly Labor Review*, LXXXVII (1964), pp. 377–84.
25. Maddison, *op. cit.*, p. 228.
26. *Ibid.*
27. The principal ones are Confederazione Generale dell'Agricoltura, Confederazione Generale dell'Industria, and Confederazione Generale del Commercio. For details of the way the wage structure functions among the largest firms, see Ammassari, *op. cit.*

series of components to reflect different circumstances changing periodically. These complexities arise, in part, because the contract must apply in so many situations and, in part, because nothing is left to the vagaries of chance.

Before the several parts of the wage package were collected together during 1954 in what was called a *conglobamento,* or literally, "a rolling into a ball," there were five separate components. Superimposed on the basic wage there was a cost-of-living supplement geared to a special price index, a bread allowance based on the price of wheat, and two increments to restore the skill differentials all but obliterated by the other adjustments.[28] In addition to these there were payments for family size, several holidays, and the traditional Christmas bonus, or *tredicesima mensilità.* From the employers' point of view there were legally required payments to be made on behalf of each worker in the form of contributions to a variety of schemes. In order of their financial importance they are old age, survivors, and disability insurance, sickness and maternity insurance, industrial accident and sickness insurance, unemployment and reduced time benefits, and aid to orphans and pensioners.

Variables of industry and location are superimposed on this package of wages, supplements, and benefits. Each industry or group of industries negotiates a contract embodying the items already noted, as well as those which are geared to the skill structure of the particular process. In addition the country was divided into four zones for wage purposes. In effect, however, because the cost-of-living allowance was applied province by province, there were ninety different geographic adjustments.

In the 1954 *conglobamento* this complex mechanism was simplified and brought up to date. For each industry group, basic rates were provided for ten classes of employees: four for workers, two for foremen, and four for clerical and executive. These rates vary with the location of the job in one of thirteen zones of the country. Quarterly adjustments in cost-of-living supplements are provided. Beyond these payments made directly to the employees, the employer must still contribute to six insurance plans which provide social benefits for his workers.[29]

Between the Northeast and Sicily these wage contracts provide notable differences in labor costs. In general, although city size is an important consideration, basic wage rates are higher in the Northeast than

28. Lutz, *op. cit.,* pp. 191–95.
29. *Ibid.*

they are in Sicily.[30] More important perhaps than the contract rates themselves, in producing higher and lower wages, is the matter of applying the rates and supplementary payments. In practice Northern firms as a whole usually pay higher wages than Southern ones. Several conditions beyond the basic regional wage differentials help to bring this about. First, there is usually greater adherence to contract rate schedules among large firms than among small ones; thus, since firm size is larger among Northern establishments than among Southern, this situation leads to a greater variation between the regions than the established rates provide. Second, Northern firms tend to pay higher production incentives than those in the South. Third, there are relatively more skilled workers, and thus higher paid workers, in the North than in the South. And fourth, because of factors yet to be discussed, more overtime is worked in the North than in the South. All of these influences tend to make the actual wage rates differ by more than the contractual rates suggest.[31]

Both actual and contractual wages are published regularly. Actual wage information is reported by the Ministero del Lavoro e della Previdenza Sociale, or the Minister of Labor and Social Security, in *Statistiche del lavoro*. Data are collected from firms employing ten or more workers. Contractual wage information is provided both by the Confederazione Generale della Industria Italiana in *Rassegna di statistiche del lavoro* and by the Istituto Centrale di Statistica in such publications as the *Annuario statistico italiano*. Wage data from both of these sources tend to be higher than the true average of wages paid in an industry or a region. In the one, the actual wages are reported by larger firms which frequently pay higher than average wages.[32] In the other, the contractual wage rates are adhered to more regularly by larger firms. Thus in both instances there is a distinct upward and sectional bias in the data.

Overlooking this disadvantage for a moment, the data prepared by the Minister of Labor and Social Security may be examined for enlightenment concerning wage levels and changes relating to specific areas of the economy. Information concerning forty-two industries from among mining, manufacturing, and utilities is reported on a monthly basis.

30. Ammassari, *op. cit.*, pp. 53–80 and 187–245.
31. Lutz, *op. cit.*, pp. 226–31.
32. Ammassari, *op. cit.*, pp. 88–91 and 177–83.

Of these, eight are sufficiently represented in most regions to provide adequate geographical comparisons. They range through the secondary and tertiary groups of industries, from such consumer-goods producers as preparers of jams and sauces, millers of cereals, and makers of macaroni and spaghetti, to such producer-goods manufacturers as makers of bricks, chemicals, and pharmaceutical products. Although these establishments often straddle the consumer-producer designation, other firms in the group—electrical utilities, graphic art establishments, and machine shops—do so more regularly. Thus these categories range broadly through the industrial structure.

Generally speaking, lower wage costs in an area tend to promote the utilization of workers there, both through the expansion of existing facilities and the opening of new ones. Wage levels in September, 1960, among the industries noted above reveal that averages of total wages in the Northeast were generally higher than those in Sicily. In Table 30 the available rates are ranked according to average hourly earning in the Northeast. In all but two of the eight cases, average total wages there are greater than they are in Sicily. In these two examples, electric utilities and chemical and pharmaceutical products, wages are higher in Sicily. The reason for this, in the latter case at least, is the extra supplement granted to these workers, for the family allowance in this industry averages forty-seven cents in Sicily to only thirty cents in the Northeast. These larger family allowances are a general phenomenon acknowledging more numerous dependents and running to three times as high for Sicily as for the Northeast.

Family allowance costs are met almost entirely by the employer and are assessed on total payroll regardless of the dependency situation of the workers in a particular firm. Payments are then made to employees on the basis of the number of his dependents. The definition of "dependents" includes, when appropriate conditions are met: wife, husband, children, parents, and even grandparents. Because family size is larger, dependency status is greater, wages on which assessments are computed tend to be lower, and payments by employers may be avoided more frequently in the South than in the North—a large transfer of benefits occurs between Northern employers and Southern workers.[33] A somewhat similar condition prevails regarding other compulsory social plans. *Ceteris paribus,* a situation of this sort, since it increases labor costs in

33. This point is developed later; see also Lutz, *op. cit.,* pp. 201–8.

Table 30. *Average composite hourly wages in selected industries and supplements thereon for the Northeast and Sicily in September, 1960 (lire)*

	Composite basic wage*		Supplement for family allowance		Supplement for vacations, paid holidays, and Christmas bonus		Total wage	
	Northeast	Sicily	Northeast	Sicily	Northeast	Sicily	Northeast	Sicily
Electric utilities	374	385	45	57	42	25	461	467
Graphic arts	295	254	16	43	19	10	330	307
Chemical and pharmaceutical products	243	227	30	47	25	35	298	309
Cereal mills	215	170	37	62	15	8	267	240
Machine shops	226	186	24	46	10	9	260	241
Brick making	193	129	38	57	9	6	240	192
Prepared foods	190	116	18	56	12	4	220	176
Pasta makers	185	147	20	60	10	7	215	214

*Including basic pay, overtime, nighttime, cost of living, bread, and other allowances.
Source: Ministero del Lavoro e della Previdenza Sociale, *Statistiche del lavoro*, Anno III, N. 1–2 (January–February, 1950), pp. 29, 30, 33, 48, 51, 53, 61, and 69; and Anno XII, N. 10, 11, and 12 (October-November-December, 1960), pp. 44–47, 52–53, 82–83, 88–89, 92–93, 108–109, and 124–25. Computations made prior to rounding. Rounding adjusted to preserve internal consistency.

the North and decreases them in the South, tends to give the South some relative advantage in employment terms.

The same generalization cannot be made regarding the supplement for vacations and holidays, or for the Christmas bonus. Differences of this sort do add directly to local wage costs. A case in point is the chemical and pharmaceutical products industry, an industry in which, it may be recalled, Italian labor costs average lower than those of other countries of the European Economic Community. The larger supplement in Sicily tends to make wages higher there than in the Northeast and so mitigates against the expansion of industrial facilities in that part of the Mezzogiorno.

Both the lowest average hourly earnings and the largest differentials between the two sections are exhibited by industries consisting of primarily local firms. On the one hand, those industries in which the predominant membership serve local markets, employ a prevailing number of workers of low skill levels, and utilize limited amounts of machinery are inclined to rank toward the bottom of Table 30. On the other hand, highly skilled and heavily mechanized groups of firms serving wide markets tend to lie near the top, with wages in Sicily at times even exceeding those in the Northeast. Part of the reason for this latter phenomenon is the necessity of attracting workers with essential skills from a distance.[34]

All of the firms reflected in these statistics had one characteristic in common: they employed at least ten workers. The multitude of small establishments, often paying lower wages, are not represented in these figures at all. The data, then, are peaks in a heavily scored landscape. The terrain grows rougher the further south one looks; agricultural wages fall away more and more from the industrial, leaving rates in commerce, transportation, and other sectors as plateaus above the valley floor of agriculture. At the same time some of the plateaus and a good part of the valleys, especially those in the South, are obscured because there are no precise data from small establishments and farms. In Sicily, for example, employment in the industries listed in Table 30 amounted in 1960 to slightly more than twenty thousand persons in a total labor force of one and one-half million, or a little more than 1.5 per cent.[35]

34. For examples of the operation of this phenomenon in the United States, see Lloyd Saville, "Earnings of Skilled and Unskilled Workers in New England and the South," *Journal of Political Economy*, LXII (1954), pp. 390–405.

35. Even including all of the workers in industries for which reports are made in *Statistiche del lavoro* only brings the total to probably not more than 2.5 per cent of the labor force. Excluded from these data are industries with less than three establishments operating in Sicily. Ministero del Lavoro e della Previdenza Sociale, *Statistiche del lavoro,*

Table 31. *Percentage increases in unadjusted and real hourly earnings in selected industries in the Northeast and Sicily between September, 1950, and September, 1960*

	Unadjusted earnings		Real earnings	
	Northeast	Sicily	Northeast	Sicily
Electric utilities	100	104	47	34
Graphic arts	83	108	34	37
Chemical and pharma-ceutical products	71	74	25	15
Cereal mills	66	81	22	19
Machine shops	56	68	14	11
Brick making	78	71	31	13
Prepared foods	74	69	28	11
Pasta makers	78	71	30	13

Source: Data from Table 30 before rounding and regional price indexes derived from *Annuario statistico italiano: 1950*, p. 321; *1960*, p. 323; and *1961*, p. 336. Weights used in constructing price indexes based on the average number of workers in these industries in their respective regions during September, 1960, from *Statistiche del lavoro*, Anno XII, pp. 44, 46, 52, 82, 88, 92, 108, and 124.

Thus, to paraphrase Lutz, these better paying firms are islands of satisfaction in a sea of want.[36]

Over the past decade, changes which brought about these present standings have been substantial. Between the Northeast and Sicily the changes in unadjusted wages clearly favor Sicily where increases in earnings were larger in five of the eight industries (Table 31). These advances, based on the total wage package, were made among firms in the upper part of the list. The industries noted in Table 30 as paying higher wages also utilize greater skills and employ more capital equipment than those in the lower part of the list. Since the industries are arranged here as they were in Table 30, according to the level of hourly earnings paid in the Northeast, there is a presumption of correlation. It is not statistically significant, however, and this amount of similarity of rankings based on average hourly earnings and changes in real wages might have occurred by chance.[37]

Movements in real wages produce a revealing pattern. They show the effect of a substantially greater amount of inflation in Sicily during the decade of the 1950's than took place in the Northeast. Be-

---

Anno XII, N. 10, 11, and 12 (October, November, and December, 1960), pp. 44, 46, 52, 82, 88, 92, 108, and 124; and *Annuario statistico italiano: 1961*, p. 332.

36. Lutz, *op. cit.*, p. 231, especially regarding the South.

37. Comparing rankings of these industries according to average hourly earnings and changes in real wages give the following results:

	S	τ	P
Northeast	+8	0.286	0.398
Sicily	+14	0.500	0.108

tween 1950 and 1960 the consumer price indexes (*numeri indici del costo della vita*) increased in Sicily by almost 50 per cent; in the Northeast they increased by about 36 per cent. As a result changes in real earnings in the two regions behaved differently from their unadjusted counterparts (right portion of Table 31). Earnings increased more than those in the Northeast in only one of the eight industries rather than in five. In the last three industries listed in Table 31—brick making, prepared foods, and pasta makers—the advances in real wages in Sicily were less than half as large as those in the Northeast. Even in the other industries, except the graphic arts, advances were substantially greater in the Northeast than in Sicily. Thus only in such exceptional cases as the graphic arts industry did hourly earnings in real terms advance more in Sicily than in the Northeast.

Under the influence of dismissal and hiring procedures, wage labor assumes some of the attributes of a fixed cost factor. Although laws forbidding firms to lay off workers are no longer in force, much collective bargaining activity has centered around this question. It has been resolved frequently by paying higher termination bonuses than provided by the contract in effect. On the other side, employers are restricted in hiring new persons. They are supposed to apply to the local employment office (Ufficio di Collocamento) for the desired number of workers of a particular skill. Recommendation by the office is based on such things as number of dependents and length of time unemployed. Rehiring requirements for old employees, termination bonuses, possible strikes, and the prevailing mores regarding dismissals operate to curb the employer's capacity to adjust his manpower to his needs. This phenomenon operates as a distinct handicap to industries with a variable demand for their product, such as shipbuilding, heavy machinery production, and others exhibiting either high seasonal or cyclical fluctuations. The effect of this practice is to reduce employment in periods of high level business activity, to increase the reliance on output incentives and overtime to provide for changes in production, and to expand labor saving devices and automation generally.[38] Because of the fixed cost element involved in the hiring of labor the enlargement of old firms and the establishment of new ones may be jeopardized.

Industrial labor costs versus agricultural labor costs and the dual labor market. Evident in Italy as in many countries is a dualism in the

38. Lutz, *op. cit.*, pp. 208–12 and 234–38.

labor market. Two distinct levels of labor are present side by side in the same locale. One is singularized by industrial skills and urban know-how, the other by a lack of training in any but simple agricultural chores and by a fear of moving from the place of birth. The rift between them applies not only to the manual dexterity and experience needed to work with complex machines, though this is formidable in itself, but also to the social intelligence required to live in a city. In Italy, where apartment-type living is the practice even on farms, one would not expect this to be a problem, but it is nevertheless. Only recently a union leader reported: "A *contadino* [peasant or farmer-like person] came to me suggesting a training course on how to live in the city before he would venture to go."[39]

Some Italian labor regulations recognize this dual situation. For example, those in the self-employed and family labor categories are not covered or are covered only to a limited extent by social security laws. They have little place in the family allowances scheme, they have less security of employment, and they have scant representation by trade unions. This condition enables many small establishments to extend, relatively, the labor factor in order to compensate for a lower per unit capital investment and thus compete successfully on the fringe of big industry. Second-class workers are also to be found among the members of labor co-operatives and artisans. Both employee benefits and employer taxes are lower among them. The basic characteristic of the self-employed, the family unit, the labor co-operative, and the artisan is one of size. Other conditions must also be met, such as the requirements that the artisan employer work manually along with his employees.[40]

The presence or absence of education and training are essential ingredients in this dual situation. The lack of facilities for industrial indoctrination in agricultural areas, the need for help from children as well as adults just to maintain life, the legal and ethnic restrictions on migration to the North or toward urban centers, and the absence of a high level of demand for workers, both men and women, in industrial occupations—all tend to perpetuate the omnipresent dichotomy between high and low paid workers. Even the employment of locally trained teachers native to the region helps to preserve the area's norms of frustration.

Organized labor and government have been attempting to reduce

39. Raffaele, *op. cit.*, p. 131.
40. Lutz, *op. cit.*, pp. 208–38.

the dual character of the labor force. As a result there has been a broadening of regulations to encompass the "small-scale sector," or "grey employment zone" as it is called. This extension of control has been more an effort to prevent big industry from securing parts and subassemblies from labor co-operatives and the like where lower wages and piece rates are in effect than in the shops of big industry itself. Companion efforts have been made to induce large firms to spread employment. One of these devices has been to impose tax penalties on establishments working employees overtime.[41]

These developments clarify the philosophy of the Italian labor movement. The goals are to furnish security for workers now employed and to provide equality for all workers. Because of the intense political orientation of unions, efforts to attain these ends have been made by political and legislative means. The result has been the careful enactment of laws at the national level covering most of the important provisions in the labor contract, wages, hours, overtime, lay-off procedures, cost-of-living bonuses, and other fringe benefits.

The "common rule," such an inescapable part of a developing labor movement, has found expression in an attempt to provide equal hours and wages for all workers. This has narrowed dangerously at times the spread of payments for skills and supervisory qualifications. It has resulted even in an attempt to narrow the spread of wages in geographic terms.[42]

By way of summary

One of the regional variables most illustrative of the standing of the labor movement in these chapters was the status of the employment of women. Large differences were found between the regional situations in the Northeast and Sicily. Table 32 shows the way these variations persist in other sections of the country. Figures here are based on the percentages of the total population of women who are in the labor force.[43]

41. *Ibid.*, pp. 212 and 232–33.
42. *Ibid.*, pp. 231–32; and Sidney and Beatrice Webb, *Industrial Democracy* (2 vols.; London: Longmans, Green and Co., 1897), II, pp. 715–39.
43. Perspective may be gained by recalling a slightly different comparison where Common Market labor forces were found to be made up of as much as 37 per cent women in comparison with Italy's 27 per cent (see p. 70, esp. n. 2).

For the Mainland regions the values vary very little from the national average of 23 per cent. But for the two Insular areas of Sicily and Sardinia the rates of female participation in the labor force are down to about one half of the Italian average. This role of women, unemancipated from the home, is evidence of an economy in which many tasks suitable for the efficient mass production techniques of the factory are still done by unspecialized household methods.

Table 32. *Percentage of women in the labor force for certain selected provinces and the regions of Italy on October 15, 1961, and probable direction of change therein since December 31, 1871*

Region Principal province Sample province	Percentage of women in labor force		Direction of probable change since 1871*
Northwest	25		o
Turin		28	o
Cuneo		24	o
Northeast	26		o
Milan		30	o
Brescia		21	—
Tuscany	21		o
Florence		24	o
Pisa		21	o
East Central	21		—
Rome		19	o
Ascoli Piceno		25	—
South	25		o
Naples		14	—
Salerno		29	—
Sicily	12		—
Palermo		9	—
Agrigento		13	—
Sardinia	12		o
Cagliari		12	o
Sassari		13	o
Italy		23	o

*o = no major change, and — = substantial decrease.
Source: Ufficio Centrale di Statistica, *Popolazione classificata per professioni, culti e infermità principali, Censimento 31 dicembre 1871* (Rome: Regia Tipografia, 1876), III, pp. 333–39; and Istituto Centrale di Statistica, *10° Censimento generale della popolazione, 15 ottobre 1961,* III, pp. 28–31.

Between the principal and sample provinces of the Northwest, the Northeast, and Tuscany, the larger urban centers of Turin, Milan, and Florence show higher labor participation by women than do the smaller sample provinces of Cuneo, Brescia, and Pisa. The reasons for this are both the greater availability of jobs for women and the greater availability of services for hire to substitute for those commonly done in the home. In the East Central region and in the South the reverse of this situation is evident. Plausible explanations for the low values in Rome and Naples are the influx of young male workers to these centers and the lack of industrial establishments there to make use of women workers. To the contrary, in Ascoli Piceno and Salerno job opportunities for women are available. The very low proportion of women working in Sicily and Sardinia is reflected in both principal and sample provinces.

Shown also in Table 32 are some very rough estimates of the direction of change in the gainful employment of women since Unification. Pronounced changes seem to have taken place in Sicily, where there has been a marked decline in the participation of women. This evidence reflects a drop in job opportunities which has been matched by a suitable alteration in the island's mores regarding gainful work by women. The participation in Sardinia measures both a modest enlargement of opportunity and a concomitant emancipation of attitude from the previous lows.

Attempts to improve the labor situation in Sicily in particular and the South and Sardinia in general have taken the form of legislative action. As a result of these efforts to control the labor market and the mores of the Italian economy, several impediments have been placed in the way of the development of the regions of the country. Low take-home pay, caused in part by the high proportion of labor costs going to social security charges, has resulted in lower worker incentives, especially among the skilled.[44] A high degree of job security produces low labor turnover, but also a reluctance by employers to chance expansion. A single level of wages from North to South provides equalitarian satisfaction, but at the same time removes a valuable incentive to the industrial development of the labor-rich South. Restrictions on obtaining parts and subassemblies from small suppliers not only provide more employment by large establishments, but also remove an invigorating source of competition with internal production. In short, the very efforts to legislate economic security may stifle employment and growth.

44. M. P. Fogarty, "Portrait of a Pay Structure," in J. L. Meij, ed., *Internal Wage Structure* (Amsterdam: North-Holland Publishing Co., 1963), p. 102, makes a point of the extreme example of the withering differentials so "that in particular cases laborers may actually be paid more than craftsmen in the same shop."

7. The supply of capital

> *The most striking thing about Tuscany is that all the public works, the roads and the bridges, look beautiful and imposing. They are at one and the same time efficient and neat, combining usefulness with grace, and everywhere one observes the care with which things are looked after, a refreshing contrast to the Papal States, which seem to keep alive only because the earth refuses to swallow them.*
>
> — J. W. von Goethe

In the field of capital improvement the Tuscan and East Central sections provide a fitting contrast. Although physically adjacent, each embodies a long tradition of distinct cultures. Divergences arose at least as far back as pre-Roman times—the Villanovans augmented by the Etruscans in one, balanced against the Picenes in the other to supply significant ethnic identities.[1] Stable Germanic joined with industrially and commercially talented Lydian countervail a martially and agriculturally strong Picene and later Roman. One recoiling from collectivist political unification went down piecemeal to the conquest of the other. Nevertheless, the talents of the loser in battle persisted and served to bolster the strength of Rome in the succeeding centuries.

Following the hiatus of Gallic conquest each region pursued its natural bent. As Roman Bishop became Pope, Rome herself advanced again to be temporal capital of the Western Church and secular capital of the Papal States. Tuscany too, was embodied in the character of a single city, Florence. Here the reality of *obesus etruscus* continued to exemplify the businessman in his triumph as entrepreneur, trader, financier, and finally consumer. His spectacular success reaped industrial and mercantile innovation and, as he became enamored of conspicuous consumption and noble symbols, a wide harvest of Renaissance art and architecture.[2]

1. Randall-MacIver, *Italy Before the Romans*, pp. 66–74 and 102–11.
2. Miriam Beard, *A History of Business* (Ann Arbor, Mich.: University of Michigan Press, 1962), pp. 124–87.

As viewed by Goethe [3] near the end of the eighteenth century, the investment in roads and bridges illustrates wider dissemination of public works in Tuscany than in the East Central region. In the first of these the long years of public appreciation for art, both as users in the textile industry and as viewers of public works and competitions, established a broad base of creative accomplishment looking toward both classical sources and future realism. In the other region, there was the clustering of specific and great artistic works in and around Rome. During the more recent past the influence of governments and war has changed the landscape of both regions. Bureaucratic enlargements have heavily influenced the economic status of Rome and the whole of Lazio, and government investments have greatly changed the economy of Tuscany. The role of the central government is present more and more in one or another of its many guises.

Italian and Common Market investments [4]

Investment rates among Common Market countries were especially high in the 1950's. In the proportion of gross national product at current prices devoted to gross domestic investment, percentages rank the Netherlands, Germany, Italy, France, and Belgium in descending order. In terms of the general effectiveness of the investment, the investment-output ratio shows the faster growing West Germany and Italy leading the other countries with substantially lower, more efficient rates. One reason for Italy's position in the vanguard was the availability of considerable excess capacity at the beginning of the decade. Even if housing expenditures are removed from the investment totals, a similar ranking persists with West Germany and Italy leading France, the Netherlands, and Belgium, in that order.

Italy's general use of investment funds follows the usual practice of the Common Market. In fact, the distributions of investments by Common Market countries according to type of activity remain notably uniform; machinery and equipment take about 45 per cent of the total, non-residential construction about 27 per cent, residential con-

3. J. W. von Goethe, *Italian Journey: 1786–1788*, trans. by W. H. Auden and Elizabeth Mayer (New York: Pantheon Books, 1962), pp. 91–100. Although his stay in Florence and Tuscany was brief, as he traveled from Ferrara to Rome in October, 1786, Goethe was nonetheless very outspoken concerning what he saw.

4. Extremely helpful in preparing this section were Maddison, *op. cit.*, pp. 76–98, and United Nations, *Yearbook of National Accounts Statistics*, especially *1964*.

struction 20 per cent, and changes in inventories a rather variable 7 per cent. In comparison with these figures Italy tends to be about average for machinery and equipment and a little high for non-residential construction. This latter may indicate an area of possible saving in investment funds by Italy's taking advantage of the usually warm climate to house heavy equipment in skeleton rather than conventionally complete buildings. Part of the high non-residential construction figure may, of course, be accounted for by the construction of dams and other extremely long-range investments during the decade. In the remaining two areas, inventories and residential construction, Italy departed a bit from the pattern of the Common Market. It was somewhat low in change in inventories and a bit high in residential construction.

Table 33. *Gross domestic capital formation and saving as percentages of gross national product*

Year	Gross domestic investment	Saving	Year	Gross domestic investment	Saving
1950	19	11	1957	22	13
1951	20	9	1958	21	14
1952	20	7	1959	22	15
1953	19	9	1960	24	15
1954	20	9	1961	24	17
1955	21	12	1962	25	16
1956	21	11	1963	24	13

Source: Yearbook of National Accounts Statistics: 1957, pp. 125–26; *1959*, pp. 128–29; *1963*, pp. 145–46; and *1964*, pp. 151–52. Concepts follow the usage of the United Nations source in which gross domestic capital formation envisages funds for homes and other structures, transportation facilities, machinery, and the like, plus additions to stocks of goods. Saving is "the surplus of current incomings over current outgoings" and amounts here to the net remaining of the capital formation after allowances for the consumption of fixed capital and the deficit of the nation on current account.

Gross domestic capital formation increased in both real and relative terms over the recent past. Between 1951 and 1960 it grew at an annual rate of 9.0 per cent, and between 1960 and 1963 at 8.9.[5] In relative terms the percentage figures in Table 33 reveal how investment has expanded from 19 per cent of gross national product to 24 and even 25 per cent. Viewed from the financing side, the allowance for capital consumption remained a hardly changing value approximating 9.5 per cent over all these years; this permitted the saving account to increase to a full 17 per cent of gross national product in 1961.

5. *Yearbook of National Accounts Statistics: 1964*, p. 371.

Generally speaking Italy was fortunate in its investment experience. Its war damage and rapid growth meant that the proportion of its gross investment going to the replacement of worn-out equipment was lower than for less damaged and less rapidly developing countries. Italy's large reservoir of unemployed and underemployed workers permitted the efficient use of much investment in capital-widening areas where product returns were most rewarding. And in technical progress Italy shared with others the advances springing out of the war. But more favorably than most of its competitor countries, Italy's high rate of investment permitted the introduction of innovations not otherwise conceivable.

Because of these very successes the immediate future may not be as bright as the past. High levels of investment during the decade of the 1950's were of major moment in the growth of all European output. Part of this expansion was brought about by enlarged international trade. Even though these existing levels may be maintained, it is questionable that they will expand in the future to give rise to accelerated investment anything like the way they have in the immediate past. The extent of capital widening will probably be reduced because the manpower pool of unemployed and underemployed now has relatively less technical competence than it had earlier. Furthermore, heavy concentrations in dams and other long-durable assets in recent years mean some reduction in immediately foreseeable capital needs. Thus, since there is a strong interrelationship among overall demand, investment incentives, and economic growth, the possibility of maintaining the investment pace of the last decade during the 1960's is remote. But what of the regional investment situation within Italy?

Regional investments

Both the fortunes of war and the design of man have encouraged investment in the South. Because of the way the battle for Italy evolved during World War II, the South made great strides forward, especially in comparison with the North. Sicily was liberated, and the Southern Boot was over-run very quickly. Then the front was stabilized on the Gothic Line, just below Rome, not very far from the line that has traditionally separated the North from the South. In ensuing months, the North was heavily damaged, bombed, and made the battlefield of German and Allied armies. The Mezzogiorno, on the other hand, was liberated and rehabilitated. Extensive durable improvements were undertaken.[6]

Among European nations the largest loans from the World Bank have been made to Italy. Designed to help the South, these loans have supported irrigation, power, and agricultural processing projects on Sicily, Sardinia, and the Southern Mainland.[7] In addition to this international investment in the region, large sums have been spent by the Italian government through the Cassa per il Mezzogiorno, mainly in agricultural, transportation, sanitation, and industrial aid.[8]

Table 34. *Investment in total, investment per worker, and investment per increase in employment for the three major sections of Italy, 1952–1961 inclusive (1960 lire)*

	Northwest	Northeast and Central	South	Italy
Investment in total (000,000,000,000)	13.1	13.6	8.6	35.3
Investment per worker (000,000)	2.6	2.0	1.4	2.0
Investment per increase in employment (000,000)	24.5	17.7	9.8	16.1

Source: Evolved from *Annuario statistico italiano: 1953*, p. 330; *1960*, p. 370; *1961*, pp. 332 and 388; and *1963*, p. 402.

In spite of special efforts to develop the productive potential of the South, experience in the decade 1952 to 1961 inclusive offered no evidence of relative gain in investment. In gross terms the Mezzogiorno gained only about two thirds as much in capital plant and equipment as either the Northwest or the Northeast and Central sections (Table 34). This comparison, because it applies to special regions with very different characteristics and population sizes, is not as precisely significant as might be desired. In this setting the Northwest comprises the

6. United States aid to Italy in the postwar period from July 1, 1945, through December 31, 1963, totaled $2,796,000,000. U. S. Bureau of the Census, *Statistical Abstract of the United States: 1964* (Washington: U. S. Government Printing Office, 1964), pp. 860–61.

7. Original principal amounts of loans to the Cassa per il Mezzogiorno by the International Bank for Reconstruction and Development between October 10, 1951, and June 30, 1963, totaled $299,628,000. International Bank for Reconstruction and Development, *Eighteenth Annual Report: 1962–1963*, p. 62.

8. The total budget voted the Cassa from 1950 to 1959 amounted to a sum of over 6,900 billion lire of 1960 purchasing power, or very roughly about ten billion United States dollars. (A convenient summary of the unadjusted figures may be found in Clough, *op. cit.*, p. 346.) The bulk of these funds, about 62 per cent, went into agriculture where much could not be considered investment since it simply went into the transfer of land ownership.

Northwest as generally used in this study plus the region of Lombardy which embraces the commercial and industrial complex of Milan. The Northeast and Central section in Table 34 encompasses the Northeast as employed heretofore, less Lombardy, plus Tuscany and the East Central section. The South is the conventional Mezzogiorno involving Sicily, Sardinia, and the Mainland south of Rome, including in particular the provinces of Frosinone and Latina in Lazio. The figures for the investment totals are in trillions of lire of 1960 purchasing power.

More meaningful are the figures for the investment per worker. Based on the number of persons in the labor force actually employed on the date of the special census in 1952, they show the amount of average investment per worker during the last decade. Stated in more easily comprehensible millions of lire, again of 1960 value, they reveal the greater improvements in the country as a whole than in the Mezzogiorno. In the industrial triangle of this broadened Northwest, investment increased by more than two and one-half million lire[9] for each worker employed in 1952. In comparison with this the Northeast and Central sections equaled the national average of two million, while the South netted an increase of less than one and one-half million, or about 70 per cent of the national average.

With a growing and shifting labor force, this view of investment based on a static population may not be as indicative of progressing conditions as one based on the actual amount of change in employment. The third line of figures in Table 34 casts the decade of investment increase in terms of the number of jobs added during the period. It shows in effect the average amount of capital added for each new worker. Broadly speaking, if these amounts were larger than the average values existing prior to the period in question, then the depth of capital has increased. Certainly the advance in the South has been much less than in the Northeast and Central sections and a great deal less than in the Northwest. Apparently the multiplier and acceleration effects of aid to the Mezzogiorno helped to induce an even greater expansion of facilities north of the Gothic Line.

To discern the realities of this situation a more detailed view is needed. One way to accomplish this is to examine just a single category of investment at a time. This has been done in Table 35 where industrial investment is arranged in a pattern similar to the one utilized in

9. Corresponding very roughly to 4,200 United States dollars.

Table 34. The employment figures used in this instance apply not to the general labor force as they did in Table 34, but only to the workers in the industrial sector.

Table 35. *Investment in industry, investment in industry per worker, and investment in industry per increase in employment for the three major sections of Italy, 1951– 1961 inclusive (1960 lire)*

	Northwest	Northeast and Central	South	Italy
Investment in total (000,000,000,000)	5.0	3.6	1.8	10.4
Investment per worker (000,000)	2.4	2.6	2.4	2.5
Investment per increase in employment (000,000)	7.8	5.9	14.3	7.6

Source: Those noted in Table 34 plus Istituto Centrale di Statistica, *Imprese, unità locali, addetti,* Vol. I of *4° Censimento generale dell'industria e del commercio: 16 ottobre 1961* (Rome: Stabilimento Tipografico Fausto Failli, 1962), pp. 10–13.

In spite of the progressively lower investments in the Northeast and Central region and the South as compared to the Northwest, some stability is evident in the amount of investment per worker. In each part of the country, new investment per employee in the decade amounted to about two and one-half million lire. Thus, on the basis of the amount of industrial employment in 1951, new investment in that sector in the succeeding decade was equally distributed from region to region.

In terms of the new jobs added in the decade, however, there are striking contrasts. In fact, on first impression there appears to be a rather anomalous situation. In the industrial triangle of the Northwest a substantial depth of capital equipment per industrial worker already existed in 1951, while in the South it appeared to be much shallower at that time.[10] Other things being equal, one would anticipate that as each new worker in the Northwest was equipped with tools comparable to those generally in use in the area, his employment would require an investment roughly equal to the average amount per worker already in existence. And this would be a much larger amount than that re-

10. Although by no means an acceptable measure of the situation, some notion of the relative standing of the North (as a whole) in comparison with the South can be gained from the fact that the total nominal capital of corporations in the industrial field was more than ten times as large in the North as it was in the South while employment in industry was only about five times as great. SVIMEZ, *op. cit.*, pp. 592 and 607.

quired to provide a Southern worker with his smaller tool kit. In other words, *a priori,* the investment cost associated with each new job in the South would seem to be lower than that required in the Northwest.

A posteriori, a very different condition prevails. As shown in Table 35, on the average, each new industrial job in the South was associated with almost double the amount of new investment required in the Northwest. Several conditions bring this about. Two of them have preponderant influence. First, in contrast with the Northwest, the industry introduced into the South during the decade tended to be more of the type requiring large amounts of investment per employee. Steel mills at Bagnoli and Taranto and oil refineries at Augusta and Gela are continuing cases in point. Special locational advantages dictate the choice of investments of this type and attractive financing terms [11] help to make them feasible there.

And second, new industrial firms which employ modern, automatic machinery were established in the South. Much of the technical processes of such plants as the electro-mechanical works at Praia a Mare and the woolen mill at Foggia are built into the equipment. The scarcity of skilled labor and the availability of low cost financing dictate the use of more capital per worker in the South than in the Northwest. This evidence supports the thesis that to increase employment in an underdeveloped area by industrial investment is an extremely expensive undertaking.

The investment in public works is also illuminating. In this instance, total expenditures during the decade in the Northwest were just about half of those in the other two areas (Table 36). Even in per capita terms the Northwest fared less well than the rest of the country which received a surprisingly uniform third again as much. In terms of population growth much the same picture is evident. The relative improvement in this instance is more emphatically apparent, however, since the flow of population to the industrial triangle of the Northwest produced a greater population gain, and so, an even smaller relative increase in public works in that area than in the other two.

A similar pattern is evident in agricultural investment.[12] In both the

11. On Sardinia, for example, the Credito Industriale Sardo, under Law No. 623 of July 30, 1959, offers loans for the construction of new industries or the development of old ones on the following terms: repayment over fifteen years, delayed for five years, and amortization at 3 per cent. In addition, locally provided free plant sites are sometimes available.

12. Also, agricultural firms in this census in 1961 reflect only a minor portion of the total employment in the agricultural sector to which the investment in question is directed.

areas of public works and agriculture there is an apparent effort by the government to compensate the other two sections for their lack of accomplishment in the industrial field. It seems almost as if the government were trying by these two programs to push the Lorenz curve of income distribution a little closer to the forty-five degree line of income equality.

Table 36. *Investment in public works, investment in public works per capita, and investment in public works per increase in population for the three major sections of Italy, 1951–1961 inclusive (1960 lire)*

	Northwest	Northeast and Central	South	Italy
Investment in total (000,000,000)	630	1,290	1,260	3,180
Investment per capita (000)	53	71	71	67
Investment per increase in population (000)	440	1,600	1,410	1,020

Source: Those noted in Table 34 plus *Annuario statistico italiano: 1961*, pp. 16–17.

A more detailed look may now be taken at the regional distribution of industrial workers. The reason for this is the possibility of obtaining a greater insight into the nature of Italian industrialization from an examination of the distribution of industrial employment and changes occurring in it recently. A variety of industrial growth is evident. Some specific areas fared significantly better than others. Table 37 also shows the preponderance of industrial employment in the North. Some three and one-half million workers lived north of the Gothic Line, while less than three quarters of a million were located south of it. With industrial investment distributed in this general way, coupled with the lower job productivity of Southern investment already noted, the results were a much greater expansion in industrial employment in the North than in the South. Although the Northwest (including this time only the Piedmont, the Valley of Aosta, and Liguria), the South, Sicily, and Sardinia netted considerably less than the rest of Italy, it was Sardinia that actually had fewer industrial workers in 1961 than ten years earlier.

In general, the smaller sample provinces fared little worse and sometimes even better than the principal provinces of the regions. Ascoli Piceno expanded more than Rome, and Sassari more than Cagliari. But these differences are based largely on smaller situations where the advent of a few new firms might easily spell the difference between expansion and contraction. The two sample provinces of particular interest in the present comparison are Pisa from Tuscany and Ascoli Piceno from the East Central region. A further look at the source of their particular success is in order.

Table 37. *Industrial employment in 1951 and percentage change therein between 1951 and 1961 for the regions, principal provinces, and sample provinces of Italy*

Region
  Principal province
  Sample province
	Employment in 1951
	(000)
			Change in employment
			1951–1961 (%)	

Northwest	831		+23	
Turin		330		+36
Cuneo		40		+32
Northeast	2,024		+41	
Milan		639		+44
Brescia		78		+40
Tuscany	301		+45	
Florence		105		+58
Pisa		33		+55
East Central	353		+29	
Rome		166		+30
Ascoli Piceno		16		+74
South	500		+19	
Naples		117		+42
Salerno		47		+17
Sicily	165		+14	
Palermo		39		+32
Agrigento		17		− 9
Sardinia	69		− 2	
Cagliari		48		−11
Sassari		13		+28
Italy	4,243		+33	

Source: *4° Censimento generale dell'industria e del commercio, 16 ottobre 1961*, I, pp. 10–13.

Starting with an almost equal employment base at the beginning of the decade, Tuscan manufacturing plants expanded more rapidly than those in the East Central section. In one, employment expanded by one half while in the other there was a more modest improvement; although size of firms increased in both areas, those in Tuscany maintained their lead over those in Ascoli Piceno (Table 38). At the beginning of the period in 1951 the establishments in Tuscany were fewer in number but substantially larger in size: 6 per cent employed eleven or more workers, while in the East Central section only 3 per cent employed this number. In effect, the size distribution of plants in the East Central sec-

Table 38. Percentage distributions of plants in the manufacturing sector according to number of employees in each plant for Tuscany and East Central sections and Pisa and Ascoli Piceno provinces during 1951 and 1961, and changes taking place between these years

	1951		1961		Change in percentage points and actual numbers	
	Tuscany	East Central	Tuscany	East Central	Tuscany	East Central
Percentage of employees in plant						
11 and over	6	3	10	6	+4	+3
6 to 10	5	3	9	6	+4	+3
3 to 5	14	14	20	18	+6	+4
0 to 2	75	80	61	70	−14	−10
Total	100	100	100	100		
Total number of plants (000)	44	64	51	63	+7	−1
Total number of employees (000)	238	237	351	319	+113	+82

	1951		1961		Change in percentage points and actual numbers	
	Pisa	Ascoli Piceno	Pisa	Ascoli Piceno	Pisa	Ascoli Piceno
Percentage of employees in plant						
11 and over	5	2	9	6	+4	+4
6 to 10	4	3	10	8	+6	+5
3 to 5	13	13	22	16	+9	+3
0 to 2	78	82	59	70	−19	−12
Total	100	100	100	100		
Total number of plants (000)	6	6	5	6	−1	0
Total number of employees (000)	28	13	42	21	+14	+8

Source: Istituto Centrale di Statistica, Dati generali riassuntivi, Vol. XVII of III Censimento generale dell'industria e del commercio: 5 novembre 1951 (Rome: Stabilimento Tipografico Fausto Failli, 1957), pp. 165 and 180; and Istituto Centrale di Statistica, 4 Censimento generale dell'industria e del commercio, 16 ottobre 1961, I, pp. 30, 55, and 59.

tion at the end of the period in 1961 corresponded roughly to the distribution in Tuscany at the beginning of the period. This increase in average size and expansion of facilities in Tuscany suggests a greater ability to secure and utilize investment funds there than in the East Central section.

Turning to the sample provinces of these sections, a somewhat different pattern emerges. At both the beginning and the end of the period, Pisa had about twice as many employees as Ascoli Piceno. Though Pisa started from a higher base, its expansion in employees was smaller than its rival's. In particular, a larger unit size persisted in Pisa.

Over a larger period, looking back some seventy years, Pisa edges Ascoli Piceno in gains in total industrial employment to have more than two and one-half times as many people working in this sector now, while Ascoli Piceno has slightly more than doubled her force. The evidence for the textile component of manufacturing production shows Pisa to have had a slightly smaller decline in employment.[13] The overall development is clear: the size of each industrial unit tends to be larger, and in specific examples the employment seems to grow more or to decline less in Pisa and Tuscany than in Ascoli Piceno and the East Central section.

Part of the reason for this lies in the economic mores that were well established when Goethe visited the areas. Part stems from a variety of other influences affecting regional growth. One influence in particular is the local availability of investment funds, a factor of definite moment where so many of the local manufacturing units are small and independent.[14]

Sources of investment funds

Investment funds in the private sector are derived from the usual sources of retained earnings, individual savings, and government support. Mingling public funds with private is very much a part of the

13. According to the Direzione Generale della Statistica in *Annali di statistica* under the title *Statistica industriale: Notizie sulle condizioni industriali della Provincia di Ascoli Piceno* (1892) and . . . *della Provincia di Pisa* (1894), the textile industry employed 1,737 persons in Ascoli Piceno (1890) and 5,132 in Pisa (1892). By 1961 these had dropped to 780 and 2,638, respectively; *Imprese, unità, locali, addetti*, Vol. I of *4° Censimento generale dell'industria e del commercio, 16 ottobre 1961* (Rome: Stabilimento Tipografico Fausto Failli, 1962), pp. 54 and 56. The nineteenth-century figures for the textile industry do not include the home industry component of several thousand looms which was on the rise in each province at that time.

14. At the census of industry and commerce on October 16, 1961, more than nine tenths of the local units in Italy were independent firms. *Annuario statistico italiano: 1963*, p. 206.

scene, as is the employment of autonomous government agencies to further development and to provide competition. The Institute for Industrial Reconstruction, or IRI, is a prime example. Formed in the 1930's to direct Italy's principal commercial banks, it now controls these and a series of other companies including the country's radio and television network (RAI-TV) a commercial air service (ALITALIA), a turnpike system (AUTOSTRADE), and a number of firms in cellulose, paper, glass, textiles, and mercury. The IRI also manages a number of holding companies: STET for telephone service, FINMARE for shipping lines, FINCANTIERI for shipyards, FINSIDER for iron and steel production, FINMECCANICA for automobile, aircraft, railway, and mechanical equipment, and FINELETTRICA for electric utilities.

A companion organization to IRI, the Ente Nazionale Idrocarburi, or ENI, was established in 1953. Directed by the late Enrico Mattei, this oil company has been successful in countervailing the power of international oil companies and relieving Italy's critical shortage of oil. ENI has entered long-term contracts with the Standard Oil Company (N.J.) which involve discounts amounting to as much as 20 per cent and which allow payments to be made in Italian goods and services. With the Gulf Oil Corporation, an agreement has been made to buy crude oil and to take over control of the Ragusa field in Sicily. And, with the Soviet Union, an arrangement has been negotiated to secure crude oil over the next twenty years in volume equal to that from both Standard and Gulf. Several other agreements have been negotiated, including one with the government-controlled British Oil Company to use ENI's pipeline from Genoa to Ingolstadt, and another one to build a line from Trieste to Bavaria. In the area of exploration ENI is developing natural gas in Libya and petroleum in the North Sea, Sicily, the Indian Ocean, and Tunisia.[15] In response to the apparent opportunities in these areas, new capital expenditures by IRI and ENI exceeded 10 per cent of Italy's total investment in 1961.[16] Furthermore, the direction of change as evidenced by the Giolitti Plan, the Saraceno Report, and the Pieraccini Plan is toward a substantial increase in investment in the public sector.[17]

Public support of private endeavor is also forthcoming, especially in

15. For an elaboration in English of ENI's many-sided activities, see Dow Votaw's analysis in *The Six-Legged Dog* (Berkeley: University of California Press, 1964).
16. Economist Intelligence Unit, *Quarterly Economic Review of Italy, Annual Supplement*, August, 1964, p. 7.
17. *Ibid.*, February, 1965, pp. 8–9.

the Mezzogiorno. While emphasis during the early 1950's was on transportation, communication, and sanitation, latterly the stress has shifted from "social fixed capital" to investment in private industry.[18] Government aid takes the form of tax concessions in certain areas and the availability of low interest loans generally in the South. A large number of institutes function as intermediaries between entrepreneurs and the treasury, the Cassa per il Mezzogiorno, and the money market. Biggest of these is the Istituto Mobiliare Italiano, or IMI, which had medium and long term loans approximating two billion dollars outstanding in 1963. It functions broadly, providing credit to all types of Italian industrial firms, financing the exportation of capital goods, acting as agent in Italy of the European Coal and Steel Community, receiving support from the Export-Import Bank of the United States, making loans to foreign firms for investment in Italy, and securing interest contributions from the government on new ventures in the South. Also functioning are regional counterparts of this national organization, such as Credito Industriale Sardo, or CIS, which provide development credit in their sections.

Table 39. *Percentage distribution of investments in manufacturing industry by classes of lending institution on December 31, 1958, and December 31, 1964, and changes therein between these dates*

	Per cent		Change in percentage points
	1958	*1964*	
Banks of national interest	22.0	22.6	+0.6
Special credit institutes	21.2	25.6	+4.4
Ordinary credit banks	19.3	16.9	−2.4
Public law banks	18.5	18.5	0.0
Co-operative banks	9.6	8.2	−1.4
Savings banks	9.4	8.2	−1.2
Total	100.0	100.0	

Source: *Annuario statistico italiano: 1959*, p. 271; and *1965*, p. 305.

More than one fifth of the investments in the manufacturing sector have been made by special credit institutes (*istituti speciali di credito*) such as IMI and CIS (Table 39). This amount ranks second only to the category "banks of national interest" (*banche di interesse nazionale*) which includes the country's largest, many-branched commercial banks. The Banca Commerciale Italiana, Credito Italiano, and Banco di Roma

18. Lutz, *op. cit.*, pp. 98–99.

were the ones taken over by the government in the thirties and now are numbered among the IRI organizations. Ordinary credit banks (*banche di credito ordinario*) involve some 140 establishments of corporate, partnership, and state ownership form. Public law banks (*istituti di credito di diritto pubblico*) also comprise private and state directed organizations. In addition to providing the usual services of commercial banks these large institutions are permitted to extend special industrial and agricultural credits. The last two sources of funds for manufacturing industry listed in Table 39, the roughly 130 co-operative banks (*banche popolari cooperative*) and the 90 or so savings banks (*casse di risparmio e monti di I categoria*) furnish substantially lesser amounts than the other four classes. Although they do provide roughly half as much as the others, the co-operative banks number among their members the *casse rurali,* or mutual savings banks usually managed by farmers, and the savings banks, themselves, which were derived in many instances from some of the oldest charitable organizations in Italy.[19] Clearly, public and private funds are linked at every level, often within the same organization.

Between the end of 1958 and the end of 1964 investment by these establishments in manufacturing industry more than doubled.[20] At the same time there were shifts in the relative standings of these six categories of institutions. Comparative gains in total credits outstanding were made mainly by the special credit institutes and to a lesser extent by the very large commercial banks. These two changes are in keeping with the evidence of the increased involvement of the government in industrial development efforts. Activity by IMI and IRI, for example, are reflected here. Declines, on the other hand, were registered by the more numerous and smaller ordinary credit banks, co-operative banks, and savings banks, which are essentially private rather than government controlled. Thus the public sector has been increasing its ascendancy in the strategically important investment area.

As collectors of funds, these credit institutions rank very differently from their standings as investors in manufacturing industry. Comparing Table 40 with Table 39, the special credit institutes are excluded because they do not receive deposits in the conventional sense. In a way

19. E. J. Joint, *Italy: Economic and Commercial Conditions in Italy* (London: Her Majesty's Stationary Office, 1955), pp. 5–7.
20. *Annuario statistico italiano: 1959*, pp. 271 and 297; and *1965*, pp. 305 and 332.

their place is taken by the postal savings system which accepts deposits but does not grant loans. The areas involved are different, too; in Table 39 the percentages are for manufacturing industry in Italy as a whole, while in Table 40 the focus is broadened in one direction to cover all deposits regardless of their ultimate use and narrowed in the other to cover only two regions, Tuscany and Marche. These are the regions embracing the sample provinces of Pisa and Ascoli Piceno.

Table 40. *Percentage distributions of deposits in private and public institutions in Tuscany and Marche on December 31, 1958, and December 31, 1964, and changes therein between these dates*

	Tuscany		Marche		Changes in percentage points	
	1958	*1964*	*1958*	*1964*	*Tuscany*	*Marche*
Savings banks	30.9	31.1	41.3	43.5	+0.2	+2.2
Public law banks	23.9	24.6	11.2	10.7	+0.7	−0.5
Postal savings system	16.5	12.9	25.0	20.4	−3.6	−4.6
Ordinary credit banks	16.1	16.2	11.0	9.9	+0.1	−1.1
Banks of national interest	10.1	11.0	8.7	7.3	+0.9	−1.4
Co-operative banks	2.5	4.2	2.8	8.2	+1.7	+5.4
Total	100.0	100.0	100.0	100.0		

Source: *Annuario statistico italiano: 1959*, p. 269; and *1965*, p. 302.

Narrowing the geographic range permits a closer examination of the sources of local funds for investment. Local customs and institutions differ appreciably from section to section. Nationally, the postal system held one fifth of all deposits at the end of 1958. The relative importance of this manner of saving varied widely from region to region, ranging from highs in rural areas, particularly in the South, as great as 50 per cent of total deposits in Basilicata, to lows in urban places as small as 10 per cent in Lazio. Because of the ready availability of postal offices in farming areas and the mores of using this national system, more deposits were made in this fashion in outlying sections than elsewhere. Since these savings were not invested locally by this organization but channeled to Rome to become enmeshed in a highly complex lending structure,[21] this tended to produce an adverse flow of investable funds from country to town. One measure of a changing and possibly improving situation regarding financial intermediaries is the declining relative importance of

21. An example of this sort of development in the provision of capital funds has been the bureaucratic delays encountered in putting into operation the government's 1966 program of low cost loans to private builders.

postal savings in comparison with other institutions. This is notable in Table 40; between 1958 and 1964 postal savings maintained their second position in Marche but slipped from third to fourth place in Tuscany.

Over the six years, savings banks advanced from second to first place nationally and even bettered their relative position in the two regions. Also, there was a substantial expansion among co-operative banks in both regions. Of more interest in terms of development is the role these institutions play in making these savings available for industrial expansion, especially local expansion. All three of the shifts in savings noted above, the decline in postal savings and the expansions of savings banks and co-operative banks, broaden the availability of local savings for local industry. Reference again to Table 39 suggests, however, that even these gains have not been sufficient to match the expansions of the huge government-sponsored special credit institutes and the banks of national interest and public law.

Between Marche and Tuscany contrasts also exist. Savings banks and the postal savings system account for two thirds of deposits in Marche, whereas they receive less than one half of them in Tuscany (Table 40). The effect of both of these differences would be to make less credit available locally in Marche than in Tuscany. In the case of the savings banks a smaller flow of credit is possible than in the commercial banking type institutions; and in the case of the postal savings system, the funds are drawn out of the area to be invested nationally. In terms of change, the large public law banks and the banks of national interest declined in importance in Marche while they increased in importance in Tuscany. In general, then, the structure of credit institutions in Marche seems to be less well adapted to providing money for local needs than the structure in Tuscany. Furthermore, the direction of change between 1958 and 1962 seems to have worsened rather than bettered the situation.

A closer look at these two parts of the country is possible by comparing the sample provinces of the regions, Pisa for Tuscany and Ascoli Piceno for Marche. A similar pattern appears as credit facilities tend to be more available locally in the province of Pisa than in the province of Ascoli Piceno. One measure of this exists in the distribution of banking offices in the municipalities of each province. In Ascoli Piceno at the census of industry and commerce in 1961 there were seventy-three

Table 41. *Percentage distribution of credit organizations according to number of employees in Pisa and Ascoli Piceno, 1961*

Number of employees	Pisa	Ascoli Piceno
1	69	27
2	3	10
3 to 5	11	27
6 to 10	0	18
11 to 20	7	0
21 to 50	0	0
51 to 100	3	0
101 to 250	7	18
	100	100

Source: Istituto Centrale di Statistica, *Dati provinciali,* Vol. II of *4° Censimento Generale dell'industria e del commercio, 16 ottobre 1961,* Fascicolo 44, Provincia di Ascoli Piceno (Rome: Stabilimento Tipografico Fausto Failli, 1964), pp. 22–23; and Fascicolo 50, Provincia di Pisa, pp. 22–23.

comuni; twenty-nine, or 40 per cent of them, were without a credit organization or even a branch office of a larger firm. In Pisa there were thirty-nine municipalities, but only two or 5 per cent of them were without a credit establishment.[22] It might be reasoned that the lesser facilities in Ascoli Piceno were associated with a smaller, less densely populated area, but this is not the case. The populations of the two provinces are not greatly different in size, and the density of population in Ascoli Piceno is even greater than it is in Pisa.[23] It might be reasoned, also, that there was a greater concentration of larger credit establishments with many branch offices in Pisa than in Ascoli Piceno. But Table 41 shows that this is not the case. There were almost three times as many firms in Pisa, and more than two thirds of them were of the smallest, one-employee category. Thus, Pisa, the sample province of Tuscany, would seem to have a system of credit organizations more structured to meet the needs of numerous small business units. Perhaps as a result of this situation, manufacturing industry has expanded more there than it has in Ascoli Piceno over the past seventy years.

The special case of agriculture

One quarter of the Italian labor force is engaged in agriculture.[24] This

22. Istituto Centrale di Statistica, *Dati provinciali,* Vol. II of *4° Censimento generale dell'industria e del commercio, 16 ottobre 1961,* Fascicolo 50, Provincia di Pisa (Rome: Stabilimento Tipografico Fausto Failli, 1964), pp. 50–61.
23. *Annuario statistico italiano: 1965,* pp. 10–11.
24. *Ibid.,* p. 354.

fact alone might account for the amount of attention given to the possibility of improving conditions in this area. However, part of the political interest in land reform rests on the traditional backward conditions encountered in many parts of the country. Numerous examples of the small amount of capital expenditures in farming regions are evident: inadequate housing by the cave dwellers of Matera, poor transportation by the present use of resurfaced ancient Roman roads, insufficient irrigation by the existence of rocky watercourses full in the early spring and empty in the summer and fall, and antiquated agricultural techniques by the sparse school attendance in farming areas.

Political agitation after World War II produced major pieces of legislation. Among these the national Sila and Stralcio laws and the regional law of semi-autonomous Sicily were all passed in 1950.[25] In magnitude this land reform embodies about three thousand square miles or roughly 3 per cent of the land in forests and under cultivation in the whole of Italy. Some one hundred thousand farm families including perhaps one-half million persons in all are involved in the program.[26]

In general this legislation called for expropriation of parts of large estates in depressed areas, employing extensive farming techniques, improving the land by modern reclamation methods, and building homes for farm families. Remuneration for the land was at prices based on the taxable value of the land in 1938 with payments made in 5 per cent state bonds redeemable in twenty-five years.[27] Apparently buying or expropriating this land from wealthy landowners has not provided funds for investment in capital equipment. The long-term, low-yield character of the bonds used in payment has led many owners to hold the bonds for maturity rather than to acknowledge the paper loss their immediate sale would entail. When the bonds are sold the proceeds are often placed again in land, still considered "the best savings investment, especially in Southern Italy,"[28] thereby serving primarily to bid up the price of land. Furthermore, some of the absentee owners of large estates have been impelled to spend some of these proceeds on consumption to maintain

25. For legislative details, see Mario Bandini, "Land Reform in Italy," *Banca Nazionale del Lavoro: Quarterly Review*, V (1952), pp. 10–27; and J. P. C. and A. G. Carey, "Land Reform in Italy in 1955," *Banca Nazionale del Lavoro: Quarterly Review*, VIII (1955), pp. 143–55.

26. Mario Bandini, "Six Years of Land Reform," *Banca Nazionale del Lavoro: Quarterly Review*, X (1957), pp. 169–71.

27. Carlyle, *op. cit.*, pp. 127–31.

28. G. Gaetani d'Aragona, "A Critical Evaluation of Land Reform in Italy," *Land Economics*, XXX (1954), p. 18.

their living standard during inflation. In each of these instances, the amount of productive investment forthcoming from this phase of the land reform program is negligible.

Fundamentally this reform is designed to provide a subsistence farm for each peasant family. Size of farms varies with the terrain from a minimum of about four acres to a maximum of forty or fifty acres. Concerning the two regions being examined most critically in this chapter, the average is thirty-seven acres in the Maremma section which is mainly in Tuscany but extends southward into the East Central region as far as Rome. A slightly different situation prevails in the Fucino area which lies wholly within the East Central region. Here the available land is so limited and the demand for land so great that smaller "quotas" of land have been established. These average about three and one-half acres in size and are not sufficient to support a family; accordingly, they are assigned to farm laborers with the goal of satisfying up to two thirds of the economic needs of the worker's family. The balance must be secured by other employment.[29] This need for additional income may also be true of the new owners of other farms during the first several years of their occupancy.[30]

Demand for land varies from section to section. In a sense each area is an isolated market, for the mobility of workers is effectively curtailed by the selection process which provides substantial priorities to workers already attached to the soil in question or at least to those in the district in which it lies. Basically the alternative employment opportunities open to the individual will determine his choice; the mere ownership of a small farm paid for over thirty years is no guarantee of his acceptance of this way of life.

Many factors enter into his decision: (1) His earning as a day worker on someone else's farm and what he can anticipate as the proprietor of his own establishment may not be very different. He may rationalize with Enke that "subsistence farming by owners will occasion less output than when explicit wages are paid for hired labor." [31] Or again, he may decide with Ferrold that "earth is here so kind, that just tickle her with a hoe and she laughs with a harvest." [32] (2) Merely taking over the management of a farm may be an ordeal. To the man who has always

29. Bandini, "Six Years of Land Reform," pp. 184–89.
30. Gaetani, *op. cit.*, pp. 17–18.
31. Stephen Enke, "Labor Supply, Total Land Rents, and Agricultural Output in Backward Countries," *Southern Economic Journal*, XXIX (1962), p. 82.
32. Douglas Ferrold, "A Land of Plenty," 1859.

received daily instructions concerning his tasks and then payment in cash for his work, the problem of arranging his own schedule and budgeting his receipts for crops over a full twelve months is a traumatic eventuality. (3) The small size of the farm and the fixed character of its labor force (the farm family) make great diversification of product essential to keeping them employed throughout the year. The farmer and his family must perform a wide range of tasks on a number of crops. Consequently, instead of being able to utilize the economies of scale he is subjected to the diseconomies of extremely small scale operations. And finally, (4) participation in the European Economic Community reduces domestic barriers and although opening a wider protected area still exposes Italians to the competition of other Common Market farmers. In this situation the day worker is not always willing to exchange his relative freedom for the responsibilities of entrepreneurship. For many reasons then, the supply of small, low-cost farms in several sections has satisfied the existing demand.[33]

Numerous costs attend this program. Reform laws were designed to provide farm homesteads rather than to improve the efficiency of Italian agriculture. The units are so small that only high-cost, diversified, subsistence farming can be attempted. The price of these units is high in terms of the large amounts of capital equipment, especially buildings, needed in operations of this type.[34] Because of the subsistence character of the farms, additional government expenditures in the form of public works projects or subsidy payments of some sort will continue to be needed to carry along the less successful farmers.[35] And in establishing this program a new, substantial, and costly bureaucracy has been created to administer the plan. The largest cost, however, is the requirement that less than the best available agricultural techniques be employed. Almost two hundred years ago Adam Smith made the point that division of labor and specialization were the keys to improved productivity. Looking at Western economic development more recently Odd Aukrust concluded that growth is achieved more by the use of better techniques than it is by the employment of more machines.[36] Thus the greatest gains in most fields of production, especially at the earlier stages of development, seem to come from improvements

33. Bandini, "Six Years of Land Reform," pp. 176–82.
34. D'Aragona, *op. cit.*, p. 17.
35. *Ibid.*, pp. 17–18.
36. Odd Aukrust, "Factors of Economic Development: A Review of Recent Research," *Weltwirtschaftliches Archiv*, XCIII (1964), pp. 23–41.

in how the thing is done rather than with what equipment it is produced. Agriculture seems to be no exception. By substituting the best means of cultivation and adding only a very modest increase in capital equipment, specialists maintain that outputs can be substantially enlarged and living standards improved.[37] One of the surer guides to increased production is to take advantage of economies of scale and to use the farm of ideal size in each location. This does not mean that a great deal of mechanization is needed; quite to the contrary, in Italian rural areas with high population densities an intensive use of labor is clearly indicated—but on crops and fields of efficient size. With subsistence farms and small "quotas," many of the better techniques associated with scale cannot be utilized. Thus, one of the prime costs of the reform program is its concentration on small-scale, high-cost means of production that preclude the use of the best techniques.

The general case of education

Improving human resources by education is one of the prime facets of investment for development. Discovering and spreading information about new agricultural, commercial, and industrial techniques, as well as providing the populace with an expanding fund of general knowledge and progressively improved particular skills for reasoning, are all essential parts of an educational system. The necessity of this human improvement to provide an intelligent electorate, a competent labor force, and knowledgeable consumers is evident. More specific to the problem of economic development is the pivotal role played by the wider use of the better means of production. Moreover, conditioning the community to accept the new and the different is essential for progress of every sort.

One measure of the investment being made to better the labor and the intellectual potential is the number of classrooms made available for elementary students. Over the last several years at least this number has been increasing, and increasing at a more rapid rate than the number of students to people them. The resulting decline in the average number of pupils per room is one convenient statistic of regional in-

37. For example, this observation is made by Bruce F. Johnston and John W. Mellor, referring to Japan, Taiwan, and Denmark, in "The Role of Agriculture in Economic Development," *American Economic Review,* LI (1961), pp. 566–93; and William H. Nicholls, referring to Turkey, in "Investment in Agriculture in Underdeveloped Countries," *American Economic Review,* XLV (1955), pp. 58–73.

vestment in education. As shown in Table 42, between Tuscany and the East Central regions even as late as the academic year 1963–64 there was still some difference in the availability of classrooms in elementary schools. The East Central region still showed more students per room than Tuscany, and, at least since 1950–51 this difference has persisted.

Table 42. *Average number of pupils per classroom in elementary schools in Tuscany and the East Central regions in the academic years 1950–1951 and 1963–1964, and changes between these years*

	Pupils per room		Changes in pupils per room between 1950–1951 and 1963–1964
	1950–1951	*1963–1964*	
Tuscany	28	19	−9
East Central	31	22	−9

Source: *Annuario statistico italiano: 1954*, pp. 68–69; and *1965*, pp. 103–4.

Viewed in a wider frame, a second measure of the continuing investment in human resources is the number of pupils assigned to a teacher in elementary schools. A less valuable statistic, perhaps, though substantially more obtainable than one giving the total salaries of these teachers, it is a decidedly better measure than such indicators as the amounts spent on school buildings, supplies, and similar indicators of the paraphernalia associated with education. Commonly available student-teacher ratios show Italy to be a close second to Belgium among the Common Market countries having the smallest number of students in each teacher's care. Although the overall figures for the recent past suggest no general decline in classroom size among these countries, both Belgium and Italy have succeeded in lowering their averages recently and thus have even bettered their preferred positions.[38]

Within Italy these figures reveal a general improvement throughout the country. Even though these averages do not show the quality of the teachers, the length of the school year, the regularity of attendance, or the scope of the curriculum, they do give a measure of an expanded investment in education. Examined in Table 43, they indicate that the Northwest region has had the lowest averages from 1935–36 at least

38. *Statistical Abstract of the United States: 1961*, p. 942; and *1963*, p. 936. Since population densities do not vary markedly from region to region, differences in student-teacher ratios do not seem to be influenced greatly by the presence of small rural schools. The data point in the opposite direction, in fact, and Sardinia with the smallest density of population has the largest student-teacher ratios.

through 1951–52. These class sizes for elementary schools show the other regions of the North approaching, equaling, or even bettering the experience of the Northwest by 1963–64. Improvements abound over time and in each section, presumably reflecting gains in the quality of the educational system.

Table 43. *Average number of pupils per teacher in elementary schools in the regions of Italy for the academic years 1935–1936, 1951–1952, and 1963–1964*

	Pupils per teacher			Percentage of Italian average		
	1935–1936	*1951–1952*	*1963–1964*	*1935–1936*	*1951–1952*	*1963–1964*
Northwest	32	21	20	76	79	94
Northeast	46	26	21	109	100	98
Tuscany	44	22	17	105	86	79
East Central	40	23	20	94	90	91
South	44	30	24	103	113	110
Sicily	40	27	23	94	101	106
Sardinia	46	34	23	109	130	108
Italy	42	26	22	100	100	100
Mean departure of regional rates from national average				9	13	9

Note: Percentages and means computed prior to rounding.
Source: Annuario statistico italiano: 1938, pp. 267–69; *1954,* pp. 64–65; and *1965,* p. 100.

In these advances a North-South differential is clearly apparent. In the 1935–36 academic year some regions in both the North and South were above and some were below the national average of forty-two students per class. By the year 1951–52 no region in the North exceeded the national average while each of the Mezzogiorno regions, the South, Sicily, and Sardinia, were higher than the average. And by 1963–64, *all* of the Northern regions were below the average while all of the Southern ones were still above. Clearly the greatest changes occurred in the North, with the most improvement being shown by Tuscany and the Northeast and the largest relative loss of position by the Northwest.

In the general reduction in size of classes the disparity among the regions of Italy has returned to about what it was during pre-World War II days. In the right hand portion of Table 43 the class sizes are shown as percentages of the national average. The mean departures of the regional rates from the national average are shown in percentage points. The figure of 9 for 1935–36 indicates the amount of disparity among the regions of Italy. The 13 for 1951–52 shows some increase in divergence, and the 9 for 1963–64 reflects a return to the level of the thirties. But in spite of some improvement during the fifties, the contrast between North and South remained about as it was earlier and made the better conditions in the North and the poorer conditions in the South more consistent than they had been before. Little special aid was forthcoming to remedy this situation. In the budget of the Cassa per il Mezzogiorno in 1950 and 1952, for example, there was no special allowance for the support of schools, and in 1957 and 1959 such assistance amounted only to about 2 per cent of the total.[39]

As far as the measures shown here reveal the results of investment in education, there seems to be an absence of any relative improvements of the South in comparison with the North. This is just one of a number of significant regional differences which still persist. The efficiency of investments in creating new jobs, the use of funds to change the working and living conditions of farmers without regard to their productivity, and the very structure of credit facilities illuminate the way the government has performed in this strategic area. In Chapter 8 the role of the government in other areas will be examined in depth, showing how the persistent stultifying pressure of foreign occupations has helped to condition the people and their administrative processes at every level. Individuals there have been blinded even to the conceivability of economic growth.

39. Clough, *op. cit.*, p. 346.

8. *The role of the state*

> *The difficulty lies, not in the new ideas, but in escaping from the old ones, which ramify, for those brought up as most of us have been, into every corner of our minds.*
> — J. M. Keynes

Actions by the government influence all sectors of the economy. Not only in the conventional taxing, spending, coining, and regulatory aspects of administration, but also in the ways of doing and in the choice of standards, the state is instrumental in shaping the norms of performance and accomplishment. Sources of the Southern problem are deeply rooted in the past. An examination of development in the Mainland Mezzogiorno reveals how the course of this region's growth has been influenced by the policies of a succession of foreign governments. Some tangible evidence of the impact of these administrations may be gleaned from the way the incomes and spending of these regimes have shifted over time. Taking the revenue-expenditure aspects of government action and tracing them back for several hundred years shows how persistently regressive the fiscal policies of a long line of governments have been and, as a result, how difficult it is to change postures, policies, and practices of the bureaucracy, on the one hand, and the attitudes, reactions, and expectations of the subjects, on the other.

The changing pattern of expenditures

Dominated by no less than seven different dynasties between the end of Byzantine control (*ca.* 1000) and the *Risorgimento,* the South is a classic example of foreign rule. Spending dictated by occupying powers over almost three hundred years is reflected in Table 44. There extant records have been adjusted to modernize classifications, to make them roughly comparable one with another, and to show percentage distributions of government expenditures for three selected years. Assuming the years to be representative of those in their approximate era, some generalizations are possible. Over three centuries, debt payments declined substantially in relative importance. General administrative expenses remained at about the same comparative level while military spending more than doubled.

Table 44. *Percentage distributions of government expenditures by the Kingdom of Naples (Kingdom of the Two Sicilies) in 1493, 1595, and 1790*

	1493		*1595*		*1790*	
Debt payments	60		41		36	
General administration	18		22		20	
Government officials and royal or viceroy's household		10	6		7	
Miscellaneous expenses including castle upkeep		8	16		14	
Military expenses	15		27		31	
Army		10	16		23	
Navy		4	9		7	
Miscellaneous, including ambassadors, widows and orphans, and fortresses		1	2		1	
Miscellaneous	7		10		13	
Total	100		100		100	

Source: Lodovico Bianchini, *Storia delle finanze del regno di Napoli* (3rd. ed.; Naples: Stamperia Reale, 1859), pp. 157–60 and 358–59; Giuseppe Coniglio, *Il Regno di Napoli al tempo di Carlo V* (Naples: Edizioni Scientifiche Italiane, 1951), pp. 135–45; and Ministero del Tesoro, *Organi contabili e di controllo del regno di Napoli (1130–1860)* (Rome: Istituto Poligrafico dello Stato, 1953), p. 36. Adjustments made to modernize classifications of accounts and to render data generally comparable.

Borrowing in the management of the government's finances is of first importance. Three fifths of government spending in 1493 went to repayment of loans and interest. Most of this sum (97 per cent) was paid to merchants for current credits. Two items included in the other 3 per cent are interest due to bankers and a payment on an old loan. Presumably these monarchs, through recourse to merchants, lived at least a full six months ahead of their revenues and sought to pay back extraordinary loans from bankers, the Church, and others on a long-term basis. Over the full period shown in the table, debt payments tended to remain quite large, partly because of the sizable amount of the payments themselves, partly as a measure of the amounts of state income lost by previous vendings to private tax farmers who had purchased revenue collecting rights, and partly as a result of sums spent to buy back tax rights from these individual holders.

Second in importance is the general administration account with 18 per cent of the total. Most of this might be classified as court expense. Within the king's household, salaries are recorded for choir and musicians (from four to almost fourteen ducats per month each), guards (as low as two ducats per month), and a host of other staff members from doctors and horsemen to keepers of a great variety of birds and animals. Among the administrative officials of the government, salaries ranged from a high of fifty ducats per month paid to the king's lieutenant in charge of the department of accounts (Camera della Sommaria) to twelve ducats or less for regional justices.

A long tradition of class rigidities was evolved. Comparing salary ranges then and now suggests something of the general distribution of income. Going back even further than 1493 into the previous dynasty of the Angevins shows how the bow of the Lorenze curve seems to have bent back and forth at various times like an archer testing his strength. Only recently has it tended to straighten and come close to the forty-five degree line of equal distribution. Wide income differences prevailed in the court of Charles II (1250–1309). He and his successor, Robert, maintained an opulent retinue.[1]

Allowing for obvious variations in qualities of individuals and dissimilarities in positions, it is illuminating to contrast income differences in the court of Charles II with those found currently among employees of the Italian government. The salary of the doorkeeper, the lowest in these records, was one fortieth of that received by the grand chamberlain in 1299.[2] Today the highest paid employee, a director general of a bureau, receives an average annual salary of about five and one-quarter million lire, and the lowest paid regular worker, an attendant in an auxiliary group, earns roughly nine hundred thousand lire—a range of less than six times in comparison with the forty or possibly more times in the thirteenth-century case.[3] By the time of the Aragonese dynasty the salary range had declined to twenty-five-fold.

Under Spanish control in 1595 the salary range among employees of the government was almost forty times. The speaker of parliament at the top received 1,770 ducats per year, while a member of the cavalry at the bottom got only 45.[4] The range was still wider under the Bour-

1. Lodovico Bianchini, *Storia delle finanze del regno di Napoli* (3rd ed.; Naples: Stamperia Reale, 1859), p. 102.
2. *Ibid.*, p. 111.
3. *Annuario statistico italiano: 1965*, p. 366; in dollars about $8,400 and $1,450.
4. Bianchini, *op. cit.*, p. 247.

bons whose chief of the Department of Accounts received 3,000 ducats; his two assistants earned 1,600 each, while lower military ranks received 60 or less.[5] Here the income range from highest to lowest employee has grown to at least fifty-fold.[6]

Thus throughout the period, major class differences were evidenced by salary differentials which by modern standards are very great. In a society in which the highest governmental salary was at least twenty-five to fifty times as large as the lowest, the confines of a regimented class structure must have seemed an almost insurmountable obstacle to a person desiring change. Add to this the presence, until only recently, of a powerful and oppressive feudal organization, and the notion of personal development is rendered almost incomprehensible.

The labor factor of production was inadequately developed. By oppressive taxes, available funds were shifted to the state where they were used by king and noble for consumption and for the defense of their positions. In this way, commerce was inadequately encouraged and plant and equipment were not amassed. More important than these omissions was the failure to develop the manpower resources of the country. An example of this was the case of the medical school at Salerno; noted for its excellence as early as the twelfth century, it failed to sustain that eminence.[7] For the kingdom as a whole, low salaries and scanty facilities for education did little to alleviate illiteracy. For Naples, the capital and most populous Italian city of the era,[8] 2,000 ducats per year were included in general administration for the university. An unchanging allowance for over one hundred years, it began a slow increase in 1612 to the 6,915 ducats it reached near the end of Spanish domination.

If the university's twenty-four chairs were stable in number and the whole sum were spent on salaries, this would mean an average annual

5. *Ibid.*, pp. 348–58.
6. See comments concerning academic salaries at the University of Pavia by C. M. Cippola in *Money, Prices, and Civilization in the Mediterranean World* (Princeton: Princeton University Press, 1956), pp. 61–62; and a listing of salaries at Ferrara by L. Thorndike, *University Records and Life in the Middle Ages* (New York: Columbia University Press, 1944), pp. 360–63.
7. See Luigi Cibrario, *Della economia politica del Medio Evo* (2 vols.; Turin: Eredi Botta, 1861), I, pp. 444–45, concerning Salerno and the difficulties experienced in furthering a school of anatomy at Naples because the dissection of cadavers was considered profane.
8. Even as late as the eighteenth century Bartolomeo Capasso, *Sulla Circoscrizione Civile ed Ecclesiastica e Sulla Popolazione della Città di Napoli dalla fine del secolo XIII fino al 1809* (Naples: Tipografia della Regia Università, 1882), p. 75, reports the population to be 444,750, more than double that of its nearest competitor, Rome.

professorial income ranging from 83 ducats at the beginning of the period to 288 at the end.[9] In actual practice, since the mean was probably weighted by a few extremely high salaries, the modal salary of professors may not have been notably higher than that of cavalrymen. Under the Bourbons the university's share of expenditures expanded to 7,000 ducats. At this time, forty-four professors received salaries ranging from 60 to 800 ducats for a series of 120 lectures each year. The low end of the scale was only slightly higher than the income of a navy conscriptee, while the upper range corresponded exactly to the pensions paid the widows of army generals. Also within the general administration heading of Table 44 are found expenditures on libraries. In this category something less than 0.1 per cent was included by the Aragonese in 1493 for the cost of books purchased and the wages of scribes making copies of books in modern script at the direction of the king. Allowances for a library are also found in 1790, plus expenditures for the excavation of Herculaneum and Pompeii, a museum, and 221,000 ducats for educational purposes other than the university.

Security of private property was frequently in doubt. Especially essential in a modern industrial society is the security of private property. Where a strong tradition of the sanctity of a person's possessions does not exist, expensive measures in the form of guards, protective devices, and legal precautions must be taken. The cost of these not only reduces the amount of product consumable by society in other forms, but also worsens the competitive position of the group requiring them. Unfortunately some of the famous occurrences and conditions in the period under review tend to be negative rather than positive in regard to the tradition of private property. King Ferrante's social call to his barons after the signing of the peace treaty enabled him to murder them and distribute their estates to his friends. The expulsion of the Jews when they began to play an unwanted role in the nation's finances furnished a windfall of property to the state. At a lower level of public administration, the commentary concerning tax farmers during the early part of the period and public officeholders during much of the age is unanimous.[10] For example, as Bianchini notes in reference to the Spanish oc-

9. Bianchini, *op. cit.*, p. 251.
10. A. Balletti, "Ordinamenti finanziari nell'età dei comuni," *Giornale degli Economisti,* XXIX (1904), p. 189, points out that the conscience of the people was altered by the institution of tax farming which placed a self-interested individual in the role of tax collector.

cupation, ". . . we have a memory of frauds, dishonesty, thefts, and all sorts of illegitimate use of money during this period. . . ." [11] And even as late as the Bourbons many distinguished foreign observers such as Captain T. Troubridge and the Pagets were unanimous in their condemnation. As Sir Arthur Paget observed, "Every department of the State, ecclesiastical, civil, and military, has assumed the most untoward appearance. Instead of Religion, there is an excess of bigotry, corruption has succeeded to justice, . . ." [12] Such a tradition is not lightly altered.

Payments to the church and to occupying powers drained foreign exchange. The Pope often exacted 10 per cent of the income of each of the ecclesiastical organizations, at first for special purposes such as the crusades and later on a more or less regular basis. Lunt shows a receipt for the payment of a tenth under Clement VI in 1345, "from the chapter and canons of the greater church of Sulmona" and a letter of appointment of a deputy collector of a tenth under Sixtus IV in 1480 for the "kingdom of Sicily this side of the strait." [13]

To the conventional tithe, the monarch, holding his kingdom as a fief of the Church, added payments of his own. A receipt for this donation from Queen Joanna in 1367 shows a contemporary conversion rate of five florins to one ounce of gold. The bequest was originated by Robert Guiscard in 1059 after his capture of the Pope and was in exchange for recognition of his conquests. It was offset at times by the payment of all or part of the tenth on ecclesiastical revenues to the state. Thus, Clement in 1347 ordered six annual tenths and from this granted Joanna one half of the income of the four middle years and all of the income of the final year.[14]

Tributes varied in size with the needs of the Spanish kings. The one ordered by Spain and approved by the Neapolitan parliament on April 28, 1552, is an example. Providing for a total sum of 800,000 ducats it was payable in six installments over two years. About three fifths was assessed on the free population at roughly one ducat per family and two fifths on the feudal area at about twice the *odoa* (feudal payment to the

---

11. Bianchini, *op. cit.*, p. 236.
12. See this and other contemporary quotations in C. H. D. Giglioli, *Naples in 1799* (London: J. Murray, 1903), p. 384.
13. William E. Lunt, *Papal Revenues in the Middle Ages* (2 vols.; New York: Columbia University Press, 1934), II, pp. 129–33.
14. William E. Lunt, *Financial Relations of the Papacy with England to 1327* (Cambridge, Mass.: Mediaeval Academy of America, 1939), p. 45.

king).[15] The possessions of the Church were specifically included as part of the taxable area. Because the King of Spain needed the funds immediately, he borrowed against his prospective income at an interest charge of a reported 60 per cent and so netted roughly 320,000 ducats from the original payment of 800,000.

Under the press of demands by the Church, the viceroy, and foreign imports, it was sometimes necessary for the kingdom or even one of its principalities to resort to the bankers. A device in this event was the sale of tax rights or feudal income. Thus, in 1596 Salerno paid 2,551 ducats of gold to the heirs of Giovanni di Battista Spinola, a merchant-banker of Genoa.[16] In this and other transactions of the sort, valuable specie or foreign credits were lost. Foreign exchange could otherwise have been employed to work internal improvements or to import goods and services for economic development.

As was often the case elsewhere and in other times, public expenditures were little used in the development of labor and capital factors to increase output. Particularly wanting, except in Naples itself, was the improvement of such public works as roads, drainage, and water systems. Omissions were more telling than commissions; spending was concentrated in the activities of the king or viceroy and the defense of the administration. Although many of the standing army were quartered in cities and towns as a local assessment, there were continuing costs of equipment and additional maintenance to the state. The navy was of major importance during the earlier dynasty when the armada for a time numbered some one hundred and ten galleys. The army under Spain included soldiers from Spain, Tuscany, and Gaëta. This body represented not only the power of Spain in Southern Italy, but also, as developed in the military accounting office (cassa militare), a source of "graft of every type."[17] In short, expenditures at this time seemed to

15. This term in Southern Italy is often understood to mean the commuting of military service by the payment of a tax; in other areas the term *cavalcata* is used in this sense; see Cibrario, *op. cit.*, p. 103; and Ministero del Tesoro, *Organi contabili e di controllo del regno di Napoli (1130–1860)* (Rome: Istituto Poligrafico dello Stato, 1953), p. 29. Giuseppe Coniglio, *Il regno di Napoli al tempo di Carlo V* (Naples: Edizioni Scientifiche Italiane, 1951), p. 188, however, uses "adoa" to indicate the rate of taxation of that part of the kingdom still under feudal domination. This seems appropriate since the term appears frequently in the treasury ledgers of Salerno as late as 1763 (for example, State Archives, Naples: *Contro no. 95, Salerno, 1763 e 763*).
16. The contemporary account also reports annual fairs at Salerno, one for eight days beginning on May 3, and a second for ten days starting on September 21, attended by merchants from all parts of Italy as well as such other areas as Sicily and Greece; see Scipione Mazzella, *Descrizione del regno di Napoli* (Naples: n.p., 1601), p. 75.
17. Ministero del Tesoro, *op. cit.*, p. 32; and Giuseppe Coniglio, *Il viceregno di Napoli*

intend by military strength to perpetuate current authority and by salary example to accentuate class differences.

The changing pattern of receipts

A long evolution of income-seeking activities marks the world of the Neapolitan South. Although the kings of the Angevin dynasty in the latter part of the thirteenth century abolished much of the collection machinery of their predecessors and replaced experienced public officials and grand councils with court favorites and secret cabinets, a chief treasurer was appointed to supervise the income and expenditure of the state.[18] Although functions were duplicated and the structure of the system was administratively poor in general, the operation of the system was regulated and even participated in by the highest officials of the regime. Although it was impossible to forecast the condition of the treasury at any future date because no exact account of revenues and expenditures was maintained, the accounting organization inaugurated by the kings of Anjou marks the beginning of a system of accounts of the Neapolitan State.[19]

For the period prior to these thirteenth-century innovations, few financial records are available.[20] Under the Normans and later the Hohenstaufens economic regimentation had become progressively more intense. Price control was general as cities tried to bolster their redundant coinage. Omnipresent taxes augmented the activities of the mint. Even before Roger I, taxes had been carefully conceived and effectively applied.[21] Under the Normans, notwithstanding royal disclaimers to the contrary, they were exacted with incredible violence.[22]

---

nel sec. XVII (Rome: Edizioni di Storia e Letteratura, 1955), pp. 207-13. The persistence of these accounts including the payment for Genoese galleys may be noted from the records of 1630, State Archives, Naples: *Dipendenza della Sommaria*, Bundle 25.

18. Leon Cadier, *Essi sur l'Administration du Royaume de Sicile sous Charles Ier et Charles II d'Anjou* (Paris: E. Thorin, 1891), pp. 20–54, describes in detail the administrative organization under Charles I and argues that the changes introduced by him and the fact that vacancies existed in high offices over many years were justified in the interest of better government.

19. Ministero del Tesoro, *op. cit.*, pp. 21–24.

20. Some discussion of the earlier political organization of the area is presented by Enrico Besta, *Diritto pubblico*, Vol. II of *Storia del diritto italiano* (5 vols.; Milan: A. Giuffrè, 1949), pp. 140–41. As far as local finance is concerned for the early part of the period, see Balletti, *op. cit.*, pp. 172–89.

21. In the eighth century, before the advent of the Saracens, Sicily was the richest patrimony of the Church; it returned, with Calabria, 25,200 gold soldi each year; Lunt, *Papal Revenues*, I, p. 57. But by 1140, when Roger I began his reorganization of the Kingdom of Naples, parts of Campania near Naples, once the most fertile section of the lower Boot, had already been declared a "depressed area" for taxation purposes. As Whyte has forcefully stated, the subjects of the region were "abject and utterly ignorant,

Table 45. *Percentage distributions of receipts by the Kingdom of Naples (Kingdom of the Two Sicilies) in 1595 and 1790*

	1595		1790	
Direct	43		23	
Hearth and contribution		33		
Property				12
Feudal		2		2
Miscellaneous (including lodging of Spanish troops in 1595)		8		9
Indirect	28		32	
Sales		17		16
Customs and excise		11		10
Miscellaneous				6
State monopolies	3		5	
Rent of state land		1		2
Sales of goods and animals				2
Miscellaneous (including sales of offices in 1595 and income from property of expelled Jews in 1790)		2		1
Miscellaneous	26		40	
Payments absorbed in operating expenses		13		6
Payments of religious organizations				17
General income of kingdom				17
Increase in debt		13		
Total	100		100	

Source: Approximation of modern classifications of accounts developed from Bianchini, *op. cit.*, pp. 327–28; Ministero del Tesoro, *Organi contabili . . .*, p. 36; and Coniglio, *Il viceregno di Napoli . . .*, pp. 135–45.

Spanish domination through viceroys produced two hundred years of oppressive taxation. This period was followed by one of reforms introduced by Don Carlos and the Bourbon dynasty. Some differences between the two administrations are evident in the summary comparison of the revenue structure of the kingdom under the viceroys in 1595 and under the Bourbons in 1790 as shown in Table 45. Direct taxes make up two fifths of the total in the earlier year.[23] All of these were based on the hearth tax system under which each family paid exactly the same amount regardless of its size or financial status. The ordinary component was collected regularly and was offset in part by an allowance of salt.

living in hovels and caves, tied to the soil, without rights or defenders, they were like beasts of burden that cannot eat the food they carry on their backs"; Arthur J. Whyte, *Evolution of Modern Italy* (Oxford: Basil Blackwell, 1950), p. 6.

22. As Professor Bianchini has pointed out in his classic study of Neapolitan finances, if someone failed to pay his tax the first time a fine was imposed, the second time a hand was cut off; and, if he still had not learned, the third failure meant death. Bianchini, *op. cit.*, p. 71.

23. The classification of "direct" and "indirect" taxes follows the conventional Italian terminology distinguishing taxes levied directly on the individual from those assessed indirectly through the products he consumes.

Its rate reached a high of 4.87 ducats per family in 1642, but was reduced to 4.20 ducats after the Masaniello rebellion. Even then, almost half the sum went to the tax farmers.[24] The extraordinary tax was still added for such special events as the war against France (three tenths of a ducat per year for six years), the marriage of Ferdinand the Catholic's daughter (one-half ducat per family), and Viceroy Pedro di Toledo's factitious four tenths of a ducat per family for "salt and vinegar for the salad of the soldiers." [25]

The tax structure was highly regressive. In spite of the thoroughness of the taxing program of their predecessors, Charles I and his Angevin successors were able to enlarge and expand its coverage. They found not only the usual local or municipal tax on provisions (*gabelle*), but also others ranging from anchorage, customs, and handling fees, to grain, oil, and pasturage taxes affecting many areas of the royal economy. Nevertheless, they were especially successful in broadening the coverage to include such sectors as weights and measures, soap, mules, and timber. When difficulties arose in finding new sources, they were content to continue the old tax and supplement it with a new one or to increase the rate of the older tax for a special purpose. Thus, there was an old and a new tax on meat and at one time an extraordinary one-third added to the regular tax to raise a ransom for the Prince of Salerno.

Taxes in general were applied to most items at the time of their sale from warehouses or when carts loaded with goods passed one of the wooden barricades (*sbarre*) on the streets leading to the center of the city. Several taxes might be included in one sale—customs, anchorage, warehouse, weights and measures, indemnification, sales, and passage. Sometimes, also, taxes were levied on the value of personal property and collected as often as six times a year.

Even though the machinery was not effective in regulating the flow of public money, it was efficient in raising the tribute. Naturally it was frequently impossible to collect taxes in coin. Settlements might be made in a variety of ways, including the payment of either goods or services, the provision of food for the army, the means of transportation, or the

24. Regia Camera della Summaria, *Nova situatione de pagamenti fiscali de carlini 42 à foco delle provincie del Regno di Napoli, & adohi de baroni, e feudatarij* (Naples: Regia Stampa di Egido Longo, 1670), pp. 1–11.
25. Coniglio, *Il regno di Napoli . . .* , p. 181.

use of houses for lodgings. By modern standards, the regressiveness of this tax system is onerous. The tax base was largely either the hearth or consumer goods, mainly foodstuffs including such universal necessities as wine and salt. Furthermore, the clergy and the nobles, two of the higher income groups, were usually exempted from all except papal taxation. In this situation, almost the full burden of the civil administration fell on the poorer individuals.[26]

Feudal and near-feudal conditions prevented the evolution of a true money economy and some policies discouraged industrial development. During the six decades of Aragonese rule, a resurgence of feudalism required a major modification of government tax policy. Stemming from royal weakness at the end of the Angevin dynasty, the Parliament forced Alfonso in 1443, the very year in which he was recognized as king by Pope Eugene IV, to accede to the reinstatement of feudal control by the barons. Recalling conditions of three hundred years earlier, this one act was of paramount importance during the remainder of the dynasty. It exerted pressure for a change in the tax structure to replace revenue lost to feudal lords and caused civil strife that finally led to the murder of many of the barons by his successor.[27]

Throughout the history of the dependent South the general rule seems to have been one of regarding taxes primarily as sources of revenue. The classic example of their use in destroying the competitive position of an industry is the case of silk. The Spanish viceroy, the Marquis of Mondeyar, levied a tax on the production of silk goods. As a result of this policy the exports of the industry which had amounted to "millions in gold . . . every year" declined to virtually nothing.[28]

As economists have stipulated frequently, one requisite of industrial development is the presence of freely functioning markets. Marshall notes, for example, the importance of an environment in which the market mechanism calls forth calculation, and money itself provides a general incentive. Where the use of money is not well advanced, action is

26. Conditions during this dynasty, compounded by wars and the black death, became so miserable that the Pope even permitted the collectors of taxes from churches and monasteries to reduce the amount of the impost. Lunt, *Papal Revenues*, II, pp. 363–64.

27. Benedetto Croce, *Storia del regno di Napoli* (3rd ed.; Bari: Laterza & figli, 1944), pp. 66–77.

28. Bianchini, *op. cit.*, pp. 214–15; Coniglio, *Il viceregno di Napoli*, pp. 83–84; and J. P. Trevelyan, *A Short History of the Italian People* (Rev. ed.; London: George Allen & Unwin, 1956), p. 273.

dictated less by reckoning than by convention. Thus, "in backward countries there are still many habits and customs similar to those that lead a beaver in confinement to build himself a dam." [29]

A climate of growth did not exist. This phenomenon may be paraphrased as the attitude of the area toward change. This is probably the most significant of the conditionings imposed on the South by a long series of foreign dynasties. As a result of this experience which tended to preserve the status quo within each regime, changes seemed only to have occurred at the time power was transferred from one ruler to another. Thus major innovations in the field of public finance seem to have been introduced from without by the new monarch, rather than to have been created from within by the existing order. In support of this thesis is the evidence that large changes took place relatively early in each dynasty. Part of the explanation for this phenomenon may be that the advent of a new regime, usually preceded by war or invasion, unleashed the forces of change and Neapolitan scholars and officials were able to make improvements not possible under the older government. One example of change was the reinstatement of feudal power by Alfonso at the very beginning of the Aragonese dynasty. Another example of the stimulating effect of a new order is shown by the progressive improvements under the Bourbons in 1741, just six years after they came to power with the coronation of Don Carlos. But this is also evidence of the introduction of ideas from without, for undoubtedly the Tuscan lawyer, Bernardo Tanucci, had much to do with them. Changes in public finance did not seem to mature as the result of a carefully nurtured development; rather they tended to appear full grown as the result of war, revolution, or invasion.

These sporadic improvements were largely confined to Naples, however; conditions in the bulk of the kingdom were considerably worse than in the capital itself. Feudal lords still exacted heavy tribute from the communities under their control and were able to insure the continuation of their power by their right to appoint judges. Thus innovation, possible at times in the shadow of the court in Naples, was still improbable in the hinterland. [30]

29. Alfred Marshall, *Principles of Economics* (8th ed.; London: Macmillan and Co., 1938), p. 21.
30. See Whyte, *op. cit.*, pp. 6–7. Difficulties resulting from feudal rights are vigorously recounted by Croce, *op. cit.*, pp. 198–202.

Lacking forceful local authority, the strong sectional concentration of power and activity at Naples tended to reinforce differences between capital and country.[31] Even a knowledge of the conditions existing in the provinces was lacking. As late as the law of 1783 and the activities of the Department of Accounts in 1792, strenuous measures were necessary to obtain information concerning the topography and utilization of community land. In the field of administration, local governments consumed so much of their resources in raising taxes for the state that they were forced to borrow to provide their own services.[32] Finally, after the disaster of 1799, the government decided that something must be done to correct these and other abuses; but by then it was too late, for the regime soon became more concerned with survival than with reform.[33]

Thus, centuries of repression and restraint have led to a pessimistic and fatalistic attitude. After living and studying in a small town in Lucania for nine months, the Banfields concluded that there was some truth in Carlo Levi's view.[34] The Southern Italian is a despairing fatalist. He believes that the situation is hopeless and that the only sensible course is to accept patiently and resignedly the catastrophies that are in store.[35] The operation of the selection process of centuries of foreign domination of the type experienced here could quite reasonably have produced just such an outlook among the survivors. Furthermore, the Banfields found in the classification of stories elicited by pictures used in the Thematic Apperception Test that Southern Italians were much more pessimistic and fatalistic than Northern Italians.[36] Both of these characteristics oppose rather than support individual initiative needed for successful economic development.

Tax policies affecting both persons and industry, feudalism maintained until only recently, fear of change conditioned by previous calamities, and a resulting fatalism bred on want—all produced a pronounced affection for the status quo. In the past change had been

---

31. For example, Trevelyan, *op. cit.*, p. 289, comments, "Nowhere in Europe were the feudal dues and tolls so crushing as in the Kingdom of Naples."
32. See, for example, such records as State Archives, Naples: *Contro no. 95.*
33. Ministero del Tesoro, *op. cit.*, p. 38.
34. Carlo Levi, *Cristo si è fermato a Eboli* (Verona: Arnold Mondadori, 1965), pp. 7–8; the English edition is Frances Frenaye, trans., *Christ Stopped at Eboli* (Chicago: The Noonday Press, 1963), pp. 3–4.
35. Edward C. Banfield, *The Moral Basis of a Backward Society* (Chicago: The Free Press, 1958), p. 35.
36. *Ibid.*, pp. 110–11.

associated with rebellion, invasion, natural disasters, and the turmoil occasioned by passing the baton from one dynasty to another. The scene was re-enacted once more in World War II. What was the impact of violence in this instance?

The overall effect of World War II

Comparing data for 1940, the year in which World War II began for Italy, with information for 1950, the end of the recovery period, shows little difference in economic wellbeing for Italy as a whole. These two years, however, bridge a decade of steep decline and rapid reconstruction. In fact, if the real per capita income of each of the intervening years is plotted on a ratio scale, it appears as a rather precipitous "V" resting on 1945 (Chart 2). Thus the average surviving Italian had recovered his prewar level of prosperity by about 1950.

Table 46. *Real per capita incomes and convergence of these incomes for the regions of Italy, 1938, 1951, and 1960*

	Per capita income (1960 lire, 000)			Percentage of Italian income		
	1938	*1951*	*1960*	*1938*	*1951*	*1960*
Northwest	267	288	427	159	153	146
Northeast	213	233	365	127	124	125
Tuscany	164	185	298	98	98	102
East Central	181	175	306	108	93	105
South	91	121	177	54	64	61
Sicily	89	117	180	53	62	62
Sardinia	108	152	207	64	81	71
Italy	168	188	292	100	100	100
Mean departure of regional incomes from national average				32	26	26

Source: Table 9.

Experience varied significantly from region to region. Information in sufficient detail to illustrate this necessitates extending downward into the troubled thirties to 1938 and upward a bit into the developing fifties to 1951, but this extension adds only moderately to the levels of income that were experienced. Between these years spanning World War II, shown in Table 46, there was among the regions a generic advance in average regional income. The only exception to the general improvement is the East Central region, where because of a slow revival, Rome did not attain its prewar status until mid-1953. This actual decline plus the relative losses in the prosperous Northwest and Northeast were offset by substantial advances in the South, Sicily, and Sardinia. As a result there was a narrowing in the range of average incomes.

To measure this convergence a substitute is needed for the growth rates previously employed. Because it was a period of both decline and recovery, it cannot be described by a simple exponential trend. Furthermore, a single, summary value for the country as a whole would simplify the analysis. Accordingly a comparison is made of the amount mean incomes of the regions deviate from the average income of the country as a whole between one time and another. These figures are shown in Table 46 and are referred to as "mean departure of regional per capita incomes from the national average." Convergence is indicated by a decline in values, divergence by an increase. Between 1938 and 1951 the mean departure fell by one fifth and so reflected a marked decline in regional differences.

In the ensuing decade still other changes took place in the distribution of incomes among the regions of Italy. Comparing data for the year 1951 with that of 1960 in Table 46 reveals a substantial growth in real per capita income in every region, averaging for the whole of Italy five times as much as during the earlier period. In relative terms shifts were quite different from what had occurred before. The Northwest did continue to decline relatively and Tuscany did continue to increase. However, the South, Sicily, and Sardinia did not maintain their previous advance; in fact, the South declined slightly, Sicily only just held its place, while Sardinia lost materially. The sum of these alterations is no apparent net change. Thus the economic gap between the North and the South which narrowed perceptibly during war and reconstruction tended to remain unimproved during the ensuing peace.[37]

Current fiscal policy

By Western European standards, Italian taxes have tended to be regressive while her expenditures have seemed to be progressive.[38] Thus, in a sense, although relatively more has been taken from the lower income groups, more has also been given to them. Because of tax avoid-

37. A comparison of this type for the United States displays a continuing decline in regional differences; Richard A. Easterlin, "Long Swings in the Growth of the American Labor Force" (MS in National Bureau of Economic Research).
38. Maddison, *op. cit.*, p. 114.

ance, tax evasion, and even the tax structure itself, the incidence of the tax burden rests most heavily on those with smaller incomes. At the same time, the expenditure program appears to help the South, the farmer, and the less fortunate generally at the expense of the more advanced in the community.

The tax structure is generally regressive. The lion's share of taxes is collected by the national government. Local governments now raise less than one fifth of the total. Among them some eight thousand *comuni,* or municipalities, are by far the most influential, for they engross about three fourths of local taxes, leaving only one quarter to be divided rather evenly between the ninety-one provinces and five autonomous districts. These local taxes tend to be quite progressive, for although about two fifths of them result from a consumption tax, or *imposta di consumo,* the others are direct taxes based more or less on schedules keyed to income.

Table 47. *Percentage distributions of major tax sources of the national government in Italy, 1951–1952 and 1961–1962, and changes therein*

	1951–52	1961–62	*Change in percentage points*
Direct taxes (*imposte dirette*)	21	24	+3
Indirect business taxes (*tasse ed imposte indirette sugli affari*)	37	39	+2
Customs and excises (*dogane e imposte indirette sui consumi*)	23	24	+1
Monopolies of tobacco, salt, and matches (*monopoli*)	17	12	−5
Lottery (*lotto e lotterie*)	2	1	−1
Total	100	100	

Source: Annuario statistico italiano: 1953, pp. 368, 369, and 376; and *1963,* pp. 372, 373, and 379. Because of changes in taxes over time, classifications are proximate, only.

Taxes at the national level follow a substantially less progressive course. During the fiscal year 1951–52, for example, direct taxes involved only 21 per cent of the total (Table 47). These by and large were based on income and were progressively scaled. The greatest source of revenue in this group is the *imposta sui redditi di ricchezza mobile,* or literally, tax on income from movable wealth, which means in practice income from sources other than agriculture. Within this broad category the tax rates depend on both the size and the source of the income.

The other 79 per cent of taxes for the year 1951–52 were of the sort which tend to weigh relatively more heavily on persons with smaller incomes than on others in the society. An outstanding example of this phenomenon is the category of monopolies; certainly expenditures on tobacco, salt, and matches bulk more heavily in the budgets of individuals with lower incomes than with others, yet 17 per cent of national tax revenues was derived from this source. In a similar manner the indirect business taxes, the customs and excise taxes, and the lottery ultimately fall more heavily on those less able to pay. Thus, as of 1951–52, the general weight of taxes for the country as a whole was regressive rather than progressive.

By the fiscal year 1961–62 conditions had changed somewhat. Direct taxes had increased in importance to involve almost one quarter of the national total, and monopolies and lotteries had declined in relative importance. The net result was to make the total tax burden less regressive than it had been previously. During the same period total taxes including both national and local governments expanded to engross more than one fifth of net national product.[39] As a result, taxes became less regressive, but they also became a greater burden generally.

The expenditure structure is generally progressive. This is shown by substantial spending rates on social welfare and education presently (Table 48). At the national level these two items now entail almost one third of the national budget, or slightly more than 7 per cent of net national product. Their growth has been spectacular. Beginning with one third of this amount in the fiscal year 1938–39, they had expanded by 1951–52 to almost one fifth of the national budget, or 5 per cent of NNP.

Offsetting these expansions have been substantial reductions in defense spending and in the service charge on the debt. The first of these was to be anticipated in going from war to peace. The relative decline in interest payments has come about first by inflation and then by an expansion in the actual magnitude of the total budget. At the same time, although the public debt has grown in aggregate size, it has declined relatively to become less than one-third the size of the annual

39. *Annuario statistico italiano: 1953,* pp. 368, 369, and 376; *1958,* p. 354; and *1963,* pp. 372, 373, 379, and 384.

Table 48. *Percentages of total national government expenditures and net national product devoted to certain public functions for fiscal years 1938–1939, 1951–1952, and 1961–1962, and changes therein*

				Change in percentage points		
	1938–1939	1951–1952	1961–1962	1938–1939 to 1951–1952	1951–1952 to 1961–1962	1938–1939 to 1961–1962
			Per cent of total budget			
National defense	36	18	14	−18	−4	−22
Interest on public debt	17	6	6	−11	0	−11
Education	5	8	17	+3	+9	+12
Social welfare	3	11	14	+8	+3	+11
Other	39	57	49	+18	−8	+10
Total budget	100	100	100			
			Per cent of net national product			
National defense	11	5	4	−6	−1	−7
Interest of public debt	5	1	1	−4	0	−4
Education	1	2	4	+1	+2	+3
Social welfare	1	3	3	+2	0	+2
Other	12	14	12	+2	−2	0
Total budget	30	25	24	−5	−1	−6
Public debt	108	34	30	−74	−4	−78

Source: Statistical Office of the United Nations. *Statistical Yearbook: 1954* (New York: United Nations, 1954), p. 481; *1963*, p. 613; *Annuario statistico italiano: 1944–48*, p. 431; *1958*, p. 354; and *1963*, p. 384.

NNP. In short, the growth in the budget has been moderate and has been directed toward the social ends of education, public health, public assistance, and social security.

Beyond the totals shown here for social welfare there are other items giving rise to transfers which do not appear in the national budgets. Expenditures in the calendar year 1960 by social security agencies in Italy amounted to more than two trillion lire.[40] Of this roughly one quarter represented the state's participation, shown for other years as "social welfare" in Table 48. Excluding this amount the difference is still about one and one-half trillion lire or an amount equal to about 10 per cent of NNP. If this is added to the social welfare and education items in the budget for that year, total expenditures for social purposes amount to about one sixth of NNP.

This situation may be viewed in better perspective against the practice of other Common Market countries in that year. In each of them, the amounts paid out for social security purposes represent significant proportions of their NNP. These expenditure items include, in the countries where they are provided, social insurance benefits for sickness, medical care, retirement, and unemployment; family allowances to various categories of private and public employees; and aid to war victims, plus the administrative cost of these programs.

Table 49. *Cost of social security as a percentage of net national product in Common Market nations for 1960*

	Per cent
West Germany	17.7
Luxembourg	17.1
Belgium	16.8
France	15.1
Italy	14.7
Netherlands	12.2

Source: International Labor Office, *The Cost of Social Security: 1958–1960* (Geneva: La Tribune de Geneva, 1964), pp. 44–45, 88–89, 92–93, 120–21, 128–29, and 140–41; and *Yearbook of National Accounts Statistics: 1964*, pp. 21–23, 92–24, 101–3, 151, 181–83, and 207–8.

The scope of the substantial transfers involved in these systems is shown in Table 49. Here the nations of the European Economic Community are ranked in terms of the proportion of the country's net national product represented by spending on social security. The spread is

40. International Labor Office, *The Cost of Social Security: 1958–1960* (Geneva: La Tribune de Geneve, 1964), pp. 120–21.

great with West Germany at the top, and Italy standing fifth, just above the Netherlands in last place. In effect, the higher the percentage the more elaborate the program and the larger the influence on the economy of transfers from worker and tax payer to pensioners, unemployed, and the needy in general. One would surmise that these transfers, since they are from the "haves" to the "have nots," would tend to increase the propensity to consume. Logically the concomitant smaller propensity to save will lead to less investment, and thus to a lower rate of growth. At the same time there is an effect on the worker. Since so much of total labor cost is devoted to paying for these transfers, there is much less opportunity to offer him inducements for excellence.

The role of the government here has been to provide security and stability, to guarantee the continuation of the status quo. The price has been to surrender some incentives for efficiency and some capacity for growth. This is a very different role from that played by the Spaniards and others in establishing the mores of the South. It is, however, protective and intent on insuring the already accomplished advances at the risk of perpetuating conditions from the past. It may lead to a paradox of security: too much concern for past gains may limit future growth.

III. *In summary and inference*

9. *Ends and means*

Wisdom denotes the pursuing of the best ends by the best means.

— Francis Hutcheson

The goals

By formally recognizing space, one more dimension is added to the enigma of economic development. With this condition in mind the goals of the economy may be assumed. The single aim of expanding society's capacity to produce goods and services is often broadened to include a second end, the insurance of equal opportunity for every person. Equality in this sense is used to describe facilities and encouragement offered for the development of individual talents. Even a third target is frequently suggested, the guarantee of at least a certain minimum economic standard of life for those unable to achieve it for themselves. And, finally, to these three may be added the regional goal of improving, relatively, the general level of wellbeing of less fortunate regions so that at least within nations it is possible to provide an environment more nearly equal in opportunity.

In a sense these are conflicting ends. Evidence of associationist and collectivist experiments suggests that the loss of incentives to produce and to save associated with the adoption of a relatively equal distribution of income makes it impossible, under these conditions, to accomplish a significant amount of economic growth. For this reason, as these aims are pursued the concern for more equality in the distribution of income needs to be balanced against its influence on the growth in the size of income. Moreover, the interrelations between the two are not a simple less-of-one and more-of-the-other arrangement. Conceivably in some parts of the scale, both more equality of income and more total income could be achieved at the same time, or an opposite situation could evolve in which less equality could be associated with less total income. The purpose here is not to examine the full range of possibilities, but only to infer from the evidence the direction in which the force of the basic rubrics in the situation is being exerted.

The past

Sources of present regional differences lie far back in history. Across the entire breadth of experience, the natural, the physical, the humanistic, the social, and the economic all serve to differentiate one region from another. The great movement of the *Unità* in the last century was a rallying cry based more on a desire for liberation arising from geographic proximity than on a program founded on economic rationale. The Northwest, near France in language and custom, produced Cavour and Einaudi and is notable for its political skill, mechanized industry, and modern port. The Northeast, long under Austrian control, exhibits old and new commercial elegance in Venice and Milan plus a tradition of manufacturing success spread among a number of cities. Tuscany, birthplace of the Renaissance in banking and industry as well as art, still functions effectively in many areas. The East Central region, under the temporal hand of the Church for some six hundred years, contains an ever more bustling capital and a peninsula-spanning region of diverse accomplishments.

The South, of varied and lengthy domination from abroad, contains Naples, once the most populous metropolis in all Italy, and a people who have been so conditioned to unkind fate that they find difficulty in adjusting completely to a more beneficent turn. Sicily, removed from most of Italy by both the Straits of Messina and the rugged terrain of the lower Boot, has been governed in its remote fastness by sundry landowners and self-appointed chiefs. And finally, Sardinia, aloof from the mainland and Sicily, stands with a market restricted in scope and with information insulated from its usual percolation by many miles of sea. By unique qualities each region displays its separate existence.

With Unification trade began to spill over regional boundaries more than had ever been possible. The result was both expansion and contraction, for the lowered walls not only let trade out, but in as well. In this way the cottage industry of Central and Southern Italy was superseded by both the factory-developed North and the politically oriented trade war with France.

These developments in post-*Risorgimento* Italy gave rise to the classic debate between F. S. Nitti and G. Fortunato.[1] Crudely stated, one main-

---

1. Especially interesting were the tax aspects of the controversy and the role played by the Piemontese in seeing their tax system adopted along with the assumption of their internal debt by the country as a whole. For a brief summary in English of this exchange, see B. Caizzi, "The Main Themes of the History of the Southern Question," *Banca Nazionale del Lavoro: Quarterly Review*, XV (1962), pp. 383–410.

tained that the source of sectional difficulties was the higher tax burden placed on the South in comparison with the North after Unification. The latter argued that the origin of the difference was more deeply seated in the earlier backgrounds of the areas. Although it was neither one nor the other but both tax structure and sectional background that were responsible for the disparity, this difference of opinion emphasizes the deep-seated nature of the regional problem.

In the course of this preliminary inquiry the Northwest was used as an example for exploring the way populations have moved between city and town. It was found that there was a typical in migration of people to the urban centers and an out migration of industry to the rural areas. In light of these results, no dearth of markets capable of supporting firms large enough to use efficient methods is evident here.

Sicily and the Northeast were juxtaposed to show how the labor force has fared in contrasting regions. In several dimensions the Northeast has been progressing toward an employment structure characteristic of modern industrial nations. At the same time Sicily has digressed from this goal, especially in providing work for women. Underlying causes of these discrepancies lie in local mores originating more or less deeply in the past. Noteworthy among these sources were the influences of Unification in regulations and tariff wars, and of Fascism in educational reforms. More recently wage, hour, and social legislation has contributed materially to this imbalance.

Tuscany and the East Central region were contrasted to show the influence of investment on industrial growth. Facilities providing credit to a multitude of small firms were more adequately developed in the first region than in the second. This difference was reflected in a substantially greater growth in manufacturing employment since the *Risorgimento* in the one than in the other. Further, much more new investment was needed to provide a new industrial job in the Mezzogiorno than was required in the Northern parts of the country. This resulted from making capital relatively cheaper by subsidized loans and making labor comparatively more expensive by higher wages and less effective education. The resulting combination of factors in the South stressed the use of capital equipment obtained from the North at the expense of the employment of labor obtained from the South.

Finally, the long tradition of misrule of the mainland South was examined to show the extent of this influence on the people there. In addition, the government's role in channeling such a large proportion of total labor cost into social security plans was reasoned to act as a deterrent to initiative and thus to development. In short, these are the findings. Based on these facts and deductions, some suggestions for action are now in order.

The mechanism

Recommendations need to be couched in current, local, Italian terms. At the moment there is an existing economic and political system which functions to achieve solutions to the myriad day-to-day details of business and government. Ascertaining and understanding the complex social environments which exist at the present time are the first steps in providing a base from which to improve. Thus, the unique existing order is the starting point for any future development.

In Italy, because of the diversity of its regions, there are, in fact, at least seven dissimilar situations, each requiring separate and distinct treatment. The creation of five semi-autonomous regions is a step toward a solution. This is particularly true of Sicily and Sardinia. The other three regions, the Valley of Aosta, Alto Adige, and Friuli and Venezia Giulia, although possessing novel backgrounds, still represent a severe compartmentalization which might prove unwieldy if carried out to this extent throughout the country. The seven regions adopted in the present inquiry, or a slightly greater number if further study indicated a need for them, would appear to be a wiser choice. The point is clear; other equally autonomous regions do exist in Italy today even though they are not recognized formally as such. Also, the use of autonomy, in effect the adding of an additional layer of government in some sections of the country and not in others, seems less than logical. If the principle is valid, it should be instituted throughout.

The idea of autonomy rests on the notion that because regions diverge one from another, they require different sets of rules and regulations patterned on their own individual needs. This reasoning is supported by the evidence of the present investigation. The economics of the situation suggest that wage and hour legislation, social security requirements, and tax rates, at least, should be adjusted to regional conditions. In this way the political catchword of the "common rule" [2] which tends to produce

2. Sidney and Beatrice Webb, *op. cit.*, II, pp. 715-39.

unwanted economic effects[3] may be replaced by provisions varied to meet the requirements of the different regions which help to promote rather than hinder economic development.

In a multiregional economy the mechanism for making decisions influencing economic growth becomes even more crucial than it is in the case of a homogeneous situation. Currently in Italy the parliament, the Cassa per il Mezzogiorno, the Bank of Italy, cabinet ministers, and investment agencies all play important roles. The center of this planning is Rome. Because these decisions are made by a large deliberative body, by bankers, by bureaucrats, and by politicians, they tend to be deliberate, conservative, and innocuous.[4]

Ideally, planning would be carried out locally by groups of specialists. Local knowledge is essential for appropriate action. At the same time national co-ordination of regional policies is needed to avoid conflicting actions and to maintain a viewpoint removed somewhat from local political pressure. For example, a regionally based economic planning agency could be established. Such an agency might be governed ultimately by a small elite board in Rome whose members held office for long terms and so were free of political pressure. Under this national board, a regional board for each of the seven regions could be created. Although a few members of the regional boards might be appointed by the national board in Rome, election of a majority of the members would be by local banking, commercial, industrial, farming, and labor organizations.

Local boards would have the responsibility of channeling information to the board in Rome and the authority for originating local changes under final approval of the national board. The chairman of each regional board might meet with the national board about every three weeks to exchange information and to decide on proper action.[5]

Such a system of boards would seek to adjust the economic climate, both regionally and nationally, to achieve the goals which had been established. They would serve to emphasize the need for different policies

---

3. Joseph J. Spengler, "Cottage Industries: A Comment," *Economic Development and Cultural Change*, V (1957), pp. 371–73.

4. Charles R. Whittlesey, "Relation of Money to Economic Growth," *American Economic Review*, XLVI (1956), Papers and Proceedings of the 68th Meeting, pp. 199–201.

5. This organization is patterned on the Federal Reserve System in the United States which is a very effective information-gathering and action-taking institution, especially through the functioning of its Open Market Committee and the boards of the Federal Reserve Banks.

for different regions under a broad national design. Areas of action could be extended from less politically sensitive interest rate and investment policies to minimum wages, wage supplements, hour regulations, and the like, and eventually even to tax rates, subsidy payments, and ultimately to all of the actions by the government in the economic field. Actions of this sort are now taken by a slow, cumbersome process of committee and congressional approval, too often on a nationwide basis. The intent of such a system would not be to supersede parliamentary authority, but simply to administer such authority more effectively from region to region.[6] Although the system of boards would usurp some functions of existing agencies, it would implement the present governmental policy of decentralization. In short, some such organization as this could prove to be effective, for it is not enough to impose action from above when regional differences can be employed creatively to elicit economic growth.[7]

The policies

Population. In many ways population is the most important rubric in the situation. Larger populations function first to provide bigger markets and, consequently, the opportunity to make use of production and distribution units sufficiently large to permit economies of scale. Because there has been a large population in Italy for several hundred years, population growth has not contributed significantly in this respect during this period. Second, the population is the source of the labor and entrepreneurial factors of production. But labor is employed in conjunction with other factors, notably land and capital. In agriculture, high-cost, labor-intensive methods need to be used even in the modern land programs. In industry, the provision of tools corresponding to the existing depth of capital equipment is a drain on the expansion capabilities of the economy. In Italy, population growth over the period since the widespread use of cottage industry has been a detriment rather than a boon to the total productive potential of the economy.

Third, the population furnishes an expanding market for products of the community. But this function might better be served by enabling

6. There might, of course, be some increase in the pork-barreling of expenditures under a regional system of this sort.
7. Some argue that more regional autonomy will yield more political power to the Left. This is a short-range problem which should not be allowed to clutter the long-term goal of a more viable structural organization of the country. Furthermore, recent elections suggest that this danger is diminishing.

persons to demand greater per capita quantities of goods and services instead of compelling them to share with a growing population ever smaller individual portions. And fourth, the population serves to furnish a redundant number of workers. In so doing the status and dignity of the individual is reduced. Through lack of responsibility, the development and integrity of each individual suffers, and his capacity to operate creatively, especially in the entrepreneurial way of risk taking, is inhibited.

Regional differences are apparent. Population growth has been slowing in Northern regions, though it is still a major problem in the South. Stopping population growth by birth control is the principal means in this instance toward the end of a stable population. Emigration has not proved to be an adequate substitute. A promising note is the change in the attitude of the Church concerning this vital issue. Pope Paul VI has appointed a commission to study birth control; and three prominent churchmen, Paul Emile Cardinal Leger of Montreal, Leo Jozef Cardinal Suenens of Malines-Brussels, and his Beatitude Maximos IV Saigh, Melchite Patriarch of Antioch, made well-received statements concerning this issue before the Ecumenical Council.[8] Thus, a Church-acknowledged and state-supported program to stop population expansion in the South is a possibility of first priority.

Agriculture. If gains from the population explosion in Italy have long since been consumed by losses from its investment drag, labor force requirements in every area need to be examined with care. Nowhere in the economy is the plethora of people more evident than in the agricultural sector. This is particularly true of the farming regions of the South where much of the evident male labor force and practically all of the female labor supply is unemployed or underemployed. Conditions in much of this area of the Mezzogiorno are so barren that some parts have become in Italian eyes a veritable Siberia where political deviates may be exiled in order to expiate their sins.[9] Under conditions of this ilk an "out migration of people and the in migration of farm capital" [10] is needed. Maintaining the status quo by dividing the existing land into small tracts among the present population seems to be a less than satisfactory solution to the problem, for it provides

8. Rome, Italy, October 29, 1964.
9. Carlo Levi, *op. cit.*, pp. ix–xii.
10. William H. Nicholls, "Relative Economic Development of the Upper East Tennessee Valley, 1850–1950," *Economic Development and Cultural Change*, V (1957), p. 324.

at best only subsistence livelihoods and makes no provision for future population growth.

A better answer is the permanent reduction of the population both by birth control and by out migration. Needed in addition to these population control devices is the introduction of labor-intensive techniques to improve the productivity of agriculture at the same time that large proportions of both the male and female components of the labor force are employed. Labor-using rather than labor-saving methods are indicated, especially during the early stages of development when population growth and its results from previous decades are still the problem of first concern. During this period and in fact since ancient times,[11] the supply of cheap labor has needed to be employed as effectively as possible, *i.e.*, with efficient tools but with a maximum of labor-using and a minimum of labor-saving techniques.

Capital investment not in new homes and barns but in agricultural experimental stations and talented technicians is in order for learning how to employ labor effectively in labor-intensive situations region by region. Much attention has been given to the capital-intensive and the land-intensive cases. More effort should be devoted to learning the exact peculiarities of this third and possibly most universal situation.

Efforts should be started at once to condition both the people and the land to the reality of these agricultural economics. Fortunately labor-intensive methods in agriculture do not involve the high capital outlays they usually do in industry,[12] so that these investments both for expanded experimental stations and labor-using tools should not amount to any considerable budgetary problem. Certainly they should not be nearly as expensive as providing farm homesteads presently.

In short, the farm problem is not a problem of making more funds available to farmers, but rather of learning how to use effectively more farmers on the available soil. Once the means have been learned the problem becomes one of converting Italian agriculture to this general system adapted region by region. The usual devices of education and incentives will then be in order. The education will explain how it is done; the incentives will insure that it is done. Both the school and the

11. Courtenay Edward Stevens, "Agriculture and Rural Life in the Later Roman Empire," in Vol. I of *The Cambridge Economic History of Europe*, ed. J. H. Clapham and Eileen Power (Cambridge: Cambridge University Press, 1944), p. 92.

12. Bruce F. Johnston and John W. Mellor, "The Role of Agriculture in Economic Development," *American Economic Review*, LI (1961), p. 587 (note).

subsidy are needed. The ends should not be mistaken, nor the means. The ends are to provide more agricultural product and more employment; the means are the successful use of labor-intensive techniques with a very minimum of capital investment.

Labor. The need to adjust wages, hours, and fringe benefits to regional conditions is most pressing. Both the cry for unification and the practice of the "common rule" have made for the adoption of nationwide standards, especially in the social security field. Since charges associated with these benefits are often flat monthly fees paid by the employer, they have tended to add more to the cost of hiring a less skilful worker than to his more skilled counterpart. Because of geographic differentials in skills, the result has been to make labor more costly in less developed regions. Moreover, extending social insurance coverage to smaller firms and to underdeveloped regions tends to impede employment in these areas.[13] Ideally, social security regulations should be revised to exempt small businesses throughout the country and all firms in underdeveloped regions from paying these taxes. Practically, a subsidy by the government to pay all or a substantial portion of the employers' contributions in these two sectors is in order.

Much the same logic applies to setting wages by national bargaining. Even though skill differentials are provided in the agreements, levels of performance often are lower in the less developed region. This, too, tends to make labor costs relatively higher where, in fact, they should be lower if industry is to be attracted.

Social security provisions even tend at times to reverse the rural-urban migration. Benefit payments under the unemployment insurance program may induce a worker to move back to his native village, where jobs do not exist, rather than to stay in the urban center and search for work. Although this phenomenon helps to prevent ghettos of unemployed in the cities, it also makes for a hard core of unemployed in villages. More important than either of these effects is the fact that it reverses the desirable flow of people out of rural areas. In any case, the payment of benefits should be linked to either the active search for employment or the attending of training classes, but not to legal residence.

Regulations restricting layoffs and limiting the choice of new employees tend to stabilize employment, to maintain the prevailing hours

13. Spengler, *op. cit.*, p. 373.

of work, to bring about more overtime, to curtail the hiring of new workers, and to inhibit risk-taking expansions of industry. All of these influences stymie growth and development. Therefore, regulations of this sort should be abolished. If this is politically impracticable a much less attractive substitute would be the paying of cash bonuses to firms hiring a certain percentage of new employees and to firms reducing the length of the work week of their employees. Incentives applied to both of these situations would help to overcome the undesirable effects of this class of regulation and so produce more employment, especially in underdeveloped areas.

Such a policy of encouraging a reduced work week would tend to take effect in underdeveloped areas. There expansions in employment are feasible, and workers who had been supported by unemployment or other benefits would be given a chance to work. Higher labor costs associated with the shorter work week would have the effect of encouraging more capital expenditures designed to reduce the higher labor costs. In both instances the economy would benefit.

Professor Viner maintains, in his lectures delivered at the National University of Brazil, that if the masses of the population in underdeveloped countries were "literate, healthy, and sufficiently well fed . . . all else necessary for rapid economic development would come readily and easily of itself." [14] Something of this may be the case in Italy. Nutrients, both physical and spiritual, play a large role in conditioning the worker to his task. Incentives to enable men to work productively, wages enough to consume adequately, and education enough to reason coherently, provide the foundation of economic growth in every area.

Investment. During the Italian postwar miracle, the country as a whole grew rapidly. In spite of this and vigorous efforts to better the relative position of the Mezzogiorno, the regions of Italy did not grow closer together economically. One of the primary reasons for this lack of success was the concentration of spending on capital improvements centering first on social fixed investments and then on industrial plants and equipment. Much of this spending aided particularly the Northwest and the Northeast where large quantities of the equipment installed in the South were conceived and manufactured.

14. Jacob Viner, *International Trade and Economic Development* (Glencoe, Ill.: Free Press, 1952), p. 131.

Furthermore, the plants and factories constructed in the South, Sicily, and Sardinia were in many cases highly mechanized so that they added comparatively few jobs that could be filled from the ranks of local labor. Highly skilled technicians to repair the elaborate machinery frequently needed to be imported from the North. To make matters worse, these subsidized and automated new plants competed with labor-intensive older establishments. The result of introducing the new firm in some instances was a net loss of jobs, when both cottage and mechanized production might have existed side by side.[15]

Such a preoccupation with capital investment leads logically to the strengthening of labor's bargaining position. This follows from Marshall's reasoning that the less important the factor, the more inelastic its demand.[16] And so with automated factories: the fewer the number of workers, the more essential each one becomes. As a result of this concentration on capital investments in the Italian institutional scene, the terms of labor contracts have been strengthened to better the already preferred position of workers currently employed by large establishments, at the expense of much of the balance of the labor force in terms of both employment and wages.

Assuming that the growth process is only a matter of adding capital structures and capital equipment is too simple a view. It is in reality not only a complex process involving all of the productive and market components of society, but also the elaboration of these processes in an existing and functioning economy. Wisdom denotes in this instance the use of available resources to augment and complement existing facilities, but not to supersede them; to use capital where it will be most productive, but not necessarily in the biggest and most modern examples; to devote funds to providing incentives for the production of larger outputs of higher quality goods and services, but not to grant interest subsidies for the creation or expansion of just any capital facility; and to spend more on education to provide both more capable producers and more knowledgeable consumers, but not necessarily to elaborate physical facilities. In short, the best means involve helping an unspec-

15. Chi-Ming Hou, "Economic Dualism: The Case of China, 1840–1937," *Journal of Economic History*, XXIII (1963), p. 297. The difficulties in the way of enabling a labor-intensive plant to compete with capital-intensive industry should not be minimized. However, cottage and mechanized facilities do function successfully side by side. The cigarette industries in Pakistan, the woolen industries in Scotland, and the watch industries in Switzerland are examples of the feasibility of such programs.
16. Marshall, *op. cit.*, pp. 384–87.

tacular, existing society promote its present economy in all of its many facets.

Education. Although education is really part of investment, it warrants a heading of its own. Education here is used in the broadest sense; it includes both the formal system and all of the research, technical, professional, and cultural activities which function in society to erase old proclivities, to produce new knowledge, and to disseminate more information. Under such a broad definition it is difficult to say which function is most important. In terms of growth, probably the first is; for, to paraphrase Keynes, the greatest difficulty is to rid our minds of past convictions.[17] Or, looked at another way, the greatest cost of growth is the need to change.

Investment in education like investment in physical attributes should lead to definite and measurable returns. Apparently it does and at a rate not very different from business, for Siegel has found there to be no significant discrepancy between the returns from a college education and the direct returns from an equal investment of business capital.[18] Conceivably, returns in other avenues of educational investment may not be as great. The difficulties of converting a day laborer who is accustomed to working under direct supervision, receiving and acting on simple instructions, into a carefully calculating individual proprietor may take generations. This conversion is especially difficult under conditions either of agriculture or automated industry[19] where duties are largely repetitive.

Education in the broadest sense may also be a force for the industrialization of backward areas. It may provide in such locations the cultural advantages of art, music, and theater, found customarily only in crowded urban centers, and so convince managers of the advantages of locating there.

Also difficult is the problem of shaping age-old mores[20] into atti-

17. John M. Keynes, *The General Theory of Employment Interest and Money* (New York: Harcourt, Brace and Co., 1936), p. viii.
18. Irving H. Siegel, "The Role of Scientific Research in Stimulating Economic Progress," *American Economic Review*, L (1960), Papers and Proceedings of the 72nd Meeting, pp. 340–54.
19. Thorstein Veblen, *The Theory of Business Enterprise* (New York: Scribner's, 1936), pp. 307–12.
20. Bert F. Hoselitz, "Non-Economic Barriers to Economic Development," *Economic Development and Cultural Change*, I (1952), pp. 8–21. Gustav Schachter makes the point that "the roots of southern Italy's backwardness are anchored firmly in an archaic and intractable social structure. . . ." See his *The Italian South* (New York: Random House, 1965), p. 193.

tudes capable of coping successfully with the pressures of urban existence. One means of approaching this problem, as well as the general
one of interregional differences in customs, would be to offer financial
inducements to teachers who will work in regions other than their own.
Teaching in a region distant from their area of origin would provide
the catholic influence of cross-cultural benefits culminating in sub-
stantive cultural unification.

The conclusion

Factors of importance elsewhere are the basic rubrics of economic
growth in Italy as well. In proximate order of influence they are development of population, expansion of knowledge, and enlargement of
investment. Improvement in the quality, but not the quantity, of the
population is the primary concern.[21] This applies particularly to the
skills of the labor force as organizers and producers on the one hand
and to the qualities of the households as consumers and savers on the
other. Enlargement of knowledge vies for first place. In the Italian situation the search for new enlightenment will provide smaller returns
than the rapid dissemination and acceptance of information, especially
of a technical sort regarding the know-how of production and distribution. Expansion of capital facilities is a poor third in this triumvirate.
In fact, preoccupation with investments in physical capital alone may
slow rather than speed the process of regional development. To be
successful, future change must be an adjustment from the existing present in light of the eternal past. This implies a careful judgment in
regulating programs already in effect. Attempts to correct income differences too rapidly may retard overall development and produce in-
flationary problems. At the same time, programs should be flexible
enough to adjust both to general developments and to changes they
inspire in the economy.

Thus, the simple model employed at the outset may be used to clarify the conclusions. The factors of labor, capital, and organization
function in a relatively static environment. In an idealized, free economy the "invisible hand" in the market controls the flow of
these factors. In a real industrial economy the government modifies
these flows by a variety of policies. In Italy, much rewarding effort

21. Viner, *op. cit.*, pp. 129–32.

has been directed toward increasing the quantity of capital. It is reasoned here that *relatively* more attention should be given to the other two headings, organization and labor: organization, because additional efforts in this direction offer promise of such high returns; and labor, not only because it is being replaced by heavily subsidized capital, but also because there are still a substantial number of persons, especially in the South, who could and should work.

It is not enough to ensure that each person has the minimum of food, clothing, and shelter enabling him to maintain life. The wonders of the machine age make possible the removal of physical needs and at the same time lift great burdens from the hands of men. But in so doing, they create underemployment and unemployment, and fail to use the full labor potential of the population. This leads to social problems of every sort. The fatalism, the pessimism, the absence of civic pride, and all of the related problems found in Lucania are associated not only with the past, but also with the lack of jobs and the satisfactions gained from productive endeavors in the present.

Providing a minimum economic standard of life looks to enabling the worker to fulfill his needs by gainful, rewarding effort. The means require a greater emphasis on the individual and his self-esteem. In this way, want in its many guises may be assuaged. And income differences may be reduced, not by cutting down the peaks and ridges of the advanced, but by filling in the valleys and lifting the plains of the backward. Hopefully, too, the level of the whole terrain will continue to be raised in the process.

Index